WARFARE THROUGH THE AGES

KNIGHTS

Rosie Serdiville & John Sadler

Rosen
YA

New York

This edition published in 2019 by:
The Rosen Publishing Group, Inc.
29 East 21st Street
New York, NY 10010

Additional end matter copyright © 2019 by
The Rosen Publishing Group, Inc.

All rights reserved. No part of this book may be reproduced in any form
without permission in writing from the publisher, except by a reviewer
who may quote brief passages in a review.

Cataloging-in-Publication Data

Names: Serdiville, Rosie. | Sadler, John.
Title: Knights / Rosie Serdiville and John Sadler.
Description: New York : Rosen YA, 2019. | Series: Warfare through the ages | Includes index.
Identifiers: ISBN 9781499467697 (pbk.) | ISBN 9781508186519 (library bound)
Subjects: LCSH: Knights and knighthood—Europe—History—Juvenile literature. | Civilization, Medieval—Juvenile literature. | Chivalry—Europe—History—Juvenile literature.
Classification: LCC CR4513.S47 2019 | DDC 394'.7094—dc23

Manufactured in the United States of America

© 2019 Casemate Group

Metric Conversion Chart

1 inch = 2.54 centimeters; 25.4 millimeters
1 foot = 30.48 centimeters
1 yard = .914 meters
1 square foot = .093 square meters
1 square mile = 2.59 square kilometers
1 ton = .907 metric tons
1 pound = 454 grams
1 mile = 1.609 kilometers
1 cup = 250 milliliters
1 ounce = 28 grams
1 fluid ounce = 30 milliliters
1 teaspoon = 5 milliliters
1 tablespoon = 15 milliliters
1 quart = .946 liters
355 degrees F = 180 degrees Celsius

CONTENTS

Introduction: Of Arms and of Men   5

Timeline   27

Chapter 1:   1066 and All That   29

Chapter 2:   Kingdom of Heaven   44

Chapter 3:   Longshanks   63

Chapter 4:   Braveheart   80

Chapter 5:   St. Crispin's Day   95

Chapter 6:   Game of Thrones   116

Chapter 7:   Ivanhoe   139

Glossary   146

For More Information   148

For Further Reading   150

Acknowledgements   158

Index   159

INTRODUCTION

OF ARMS AND OF MEN

We have made a covenant with death,
And with hell are we at agreement.

Isaiah 28: 15

ON THE MORNING OF JANUARY 26, 1885, two days before his 52nd birthday, General Charles George Gordon made ready for his last formal engagement as Governor of the Sudan. The circumstances were unfortunate. Khartoum was about to be overrun by the followers of the Mahdi, a charismatic and ruthless visionary who was writing his name in the blood of unbelievers – and there were a lot of unbelievers. "Chinese" Gordon had sworn to defend the people of Sudan and ultimately, despite an epic defense, had failed. A tardy relief force dispatched by a recalcitrant government would not get through in time. There was a fast steamer ready at the quay which could spirit him to safety.

Gordon was not ready to desert those who had believed in him. There was one last service he could perform; to die a hero's death. Accounts differ but it seems the governor put on his dress uniform, loaded his pistol and died fighting, sword in hand. Lancelot himself could not have stage-managed it better: the act contained echoes of virtuous and unfailing chivalry combined with righteous martyrdom. Gordon's end carried clear resonances.

The Mahdi died soon after, though his regime would remain in place until 1898. Kitchener decimated it at Omdurman and British artillery obliterated Muhammad Ahmad bin Abd Allah's tomb. Gordon – thanks in no small part to Charlton Heston's lavish 1966 screen interpretation of the general in *Khartoum*) – has remained a legend.

"Knightly" codes stretch far back, may even be detected in Homer. The Trojan Sarpedon explains to his friend Glaucos:

> Why have you and I the seat of honour at home Glaucos? Why do we have the best portions, cups always full, and all treat us like something greater than men? And that fine estate on the banks of Xanthos, orchards and wheatlands of the best? For that we are bound to stand now before our people in the scorching fires of battle…

The historical roots of chivalry lie in a mist-shrouded Teutonic past, sanctioned and effectively annexed by the church. The ritual of knighthood provided a core philosophy and set of values that, while by no means always adhered too, furnished the mystique. This ideology, combined with long years of training and expensive equipment, permitted the mounted knight to maintain his elite and largely unchallenged status as arbiter on the battlefield – at least until those annoying peasants with their pesky longbows turned up.

Knight-service

In the year 1181, Henry II, founder of the Angevin Empire, attempted to regulate military affairs in England by statute. His Assize of Arms specified what arms and armor could be carried by each class, from gentleman to commoner. Henry III, a king totally unschooled in war who was struggling to recruit sufficient knights, revisited this legislation in 1242. He ordained those whose incomes exceeded £20 per year should be liable for knight service. Anyone who earned £15 was obliged to provide his own horses, and £2 freeholders their own bows. Forty years later, Edward I overhauled the regulations once again.

Knight-service could be commuted upon payment of a fine – or *scutage* – and there was, at this stage, no attempt to standardize kit. The militia, a homeland defense force raised within the separate counties, were also re-organised, and "commissions of array" were introduced for the first time. The county sheriffs, as "commissioners," were authorized and charged with reviewing the able-bodied men of each county and selecting a certain number from each settlement, suitably equipped according to their means, to serve in the militia. Their rations were to be funded from the communal purse. This form of conscription was never popular and was much abused – a tendency parodied by Shakespeare in *Henry IV Part 1*:

> [Falstaff] If I be not ashamed of my soldiers I am a soused gurnet I have misused the King's purse damnably.

Military service was bound into the mesh of feudalism, the complex obligations that existed between king and great lords as tenants-in-chief, and between lord and vassal. The feudal system has been likened to a pyramid, with the king at its apex and the various orders graded below, from tenants-in-chief through to the labouring classes whose obligation was to work the land rather than wield their swords. Military commitment arose from the act of homage offered by vassals to their lords. Normally, this was for 40 days each year and the inferior party served without wages. The magnate's corresponding duty to the monarch was expressed as *servitium debitum* (service owed). After the expiry of the contracted period, the vassal was entitled to expect wages. Lords might, however, continue to serve without getting cash, preferring to expect material rewards when the campaign was successfully concluded. Chivalry, after all, was just business.

The king was reliant upon the Wardrobe – which was somewhat like the modern-day Cabinet – to drive and supply his war effort. Senior civil servants, cofferers and controllers kept accurate records of expenditure, and they, or their representatives, frequently accompanied the army to keep an eye on them, bringing their own gaggle of servants, acolytes and baggage. Supply was important – all armies march better on a full belly and the effects of a shortage of provisions married to a dangerous excess of ale could be dire. For example, brawling broke out between the English and Welsh contingents of Edward I's army when they were engaged in the Falkirk campaign. Similar disturbances are recorded by the Hainaulter Jean le Bel who served in Edward III's unsuccessful Weardale campaign, nearly 30 years later.

Evesham

By the mid-13th century, the bulk of fighting in the field was undertaken by mailed and mounted knights. During the Evesham campaign of 1265 (as we'll see in Chapter 3), Prince Edward (later Edward I) faced two baronial armies; that of the older Simon de Montfort, which lay west of the Severn, and that of his son, besieging Pevensey. Edward moved fast, pinning his westerly opponents back behind the formidable river barrier

Army rations in the 13th century were usually bread and a mix of beans, peas and oatmeal – "potage." An army of several thousand men would require hundreds of tons of supplies per week, as well as fodder for horses and "small-beer" to drink.

and burning bridges. Gloucester was secured and a rebel fleet at anchor in Bristol dealt with. De Montfort the younger was hurrying westwards to his father's aid, advancing as far as Kenilworth. The Prince, then at Worcester and well-placed to strike a blow at either of his foes, beat up the rebel quarters at Kenilworth in a classic dawn raid before turning back for the decisive fight at Evesham.

It's been suggested that commanders of this era were lacking in strategic flair, but Edward's campaign would indicate otherwise. His dynamism can easily be contrasted with his father's lackluster performance in the earlier campaign leading to defeat at Lewes. As Sir Charles Oman, something of an admirer of Edward, observes, the essence of the campaign was the Royalists' success in maintaining the barrier of the Severn and in frustrating de Montfort's attempts to cross. The Prince, having kept his enemies apart, then moved decisively first against one and then the other.

Knights on the move

For rapid maneuver, mounted troops clearly had a considerable advantage. In the Middle Ages the standard tactical unit for

A **banneret** was a knight who led a company of troops during time of war under his own banner. Following Templar practice, the individual knight may have formed up with one of his attendants to carry his lance, plus a second in reserve at the back with spare horses and kit. As the squadron commenced its deployment, the squire would hand his master the lance and follow on.

cavalry was the ten-man *conroi* (a group of knights who trained and fought together). This was favored by the infamous Knights Templar, though larger formations were also coming into fashion: 20-man squadrons soon expanded into a unit comprised of 80 squires, 16 knights and four bannerets.

Chivalry might seek to gild the fog of war but, there were always practical matters to consider. Those embarking on knightly service were customarily equipped with letters of protection. These provided immunity from any legal proceedings that might arise while the holder was on active service – like James Bond, knights often had a license to kill. The Holkham Picture Bible, produced sometime in the early years of the 14th century, contains a pair of very striking images. The uppermost shows a scene of savage combat, mailed knights scrapping. The lower one reveals infantry just as energetically engaged, in a furious if less gentlemanly fracas, swords, bucklers, axes and the fearsome falchion much in evidence.

Numbers could be quite significant. For the first of his Welsh campaigns, Edward I recruited some 15,000 foot soldiers, many of whom were drawn from the southern fringes of the principality; for his later campaign against Wallace in 1298, the king mustered over 20,000 infantrymen. In subsequent expeditions, however, these numbers were significantly reduced. Poor societies couldn't support such large forces who'd strip the land of the food and fuel local people needed to survive. A contemporary chronicler has left us an image of the English army on the march during the Scottish campaign of 1300:

> There were many rich caparisons embroidered on silks and satins; many a beautiful pennon fixed to a lance, many a banner displayed. The neighing of horses was heard from afar; the mountains and valleys were covered with pack-horses, tents and pavilions.

Such a colorful vision, which could come directly from the pen of Scott or Tennyson, is highly idealized. The reality would be rather more mundane. Knights rode light horses, palfreys, on the line of march, saving their precious destriers (war horses)

Sedilia of Edward I at Westminster Abbey, erected during his reign.

for combat. The armies would tramp in a cacophony of noise and dust, vedettes (mounted sentries) front and rear. Mostly harnesses – suits of armor – were stowed, quite uncomfortable on the trail, baggage horses throwing up vast clouds of muck. The PBI (poor bloody infantry) tramped in long, straggling columns, ill-fed, ill-accoutred and swallowing the filth-laden dust of their betters.

A vast caravan of livestock; the army took its provisions along on the hoof, wagons laden with small beer, tents, cordage, baggage and miscellaneous gear. In the wake of the fighting men, a horde of sutlers, tapsters, prostitutes and tradesmen. These were essential: armorers, sword-smiths, bowyers, fletchers, coopers, carpenters, surgeons and quack apothecaries, laborers, wheelwrights and herdsmen. Armies were not welcomed anywhere and locals would, with very good cause, fear their passage, whether friend or foe.

People in the countryside lived free from the vast and constant noise of the modern world. This great, resounding tramp of the army, its volume filling and receding like the ebb and suck of the tide across an otherwise quiet landscape, must have seemed like the apocalypse. Quite frequently, it was almost as destructive. Where discipline was lax, rape and pillage could spread like a virus. The Anglo-Scottish wars from 1296 were characterized by a particular savagery that did not distinguish civilian from military: beating up the populace became an accepted tactic of economic warfare.

Into battle

Engaging in battle is, and always has been, a risky business. In the medieval era a commander had limited forces at his disposal, some perhaps of uncertain quality. A single defeat in the field could be catastrophic. Communications were dependent upon gallopers and, where possible, signalling with flags. Supply remained a constant headache. The army was habitually divided into four corps, each led by a great lord. Nobles were notoriously better at giving orders than obeying them. Even a king as famously tough as Edward sometimes had trouble keeping his gentry in order.

When the king commanded his host, he would invariably lead one division, surrounded by his household men. Once battle was joined, the commander-in-chief could do little to influence the final outcome. On the field, forces would deploy in linear formation, opposing divisions aligned; there was little scope for complex maneuver before the advance to contact. Any good commander needs an eye for ground, but the medieval general

Print featuring a horse, by Antoine Vérard. (Archivo Iconografico, S.A./ CORBIS-BETTMANN; Wikimedia Commons)

could not afford to have his reserves stationed too far distant lest, in the time it took them to come up, the day might already be lost.

A contemporary writer sums up the chivalric approach to the risks of battle:

> What a joyous thing is war, for many fine deeds are seen in its course, and many good lessons learnt from it. You love your comrade so much in war. When you see that your quarrel is just and your blood is fighting well, tears rise in your eyes. A great sweet feeling of loyalty and pity fills your heart on seeing your friend so valiantly exposing his body to execute and accomplish the command of our Creator. And then you prepare to go and live or die with him, and for love not abandon him. And out of that there arises such delectation, that he who has not tasted it is not fit to say what a delight is. Do you think that a man who does that fears death? Not at all; for he feels strengthened, he is so elated, that he does not know where he is. Truly he is afraid of nothing.

Armor

The mounted knight in Simon de Montfort's day relied mainly upon chain mail for bodily defense, together with a flat-topped helmet with narrow eye slits ("the sights"), cheek pieces perforated for ventilation, with an arming cap and mail hood (or "coif") worn underneath. His mail would consist of two garments: a long-sleeved, thigh-length shirt called a hauberk, and leg defenses or hose (*chausée*). Mail is both flexible and, when compared with plate, quite light. It may not, however, protect the wearer against a crushing blow, which can cause severe contusions or fractures even if the links hold.

That vulnerable area around the neck received extra protection from a stiff, laced collar, possibly reinforced with steel plates. Occasionally a coat of plates (reminiscent of the *lorica squamatae* of the classical age), was worn. Mailed gauntlets or mittens were carried to protect the hands. By the start of the 14th century, a man's thighs were further protected by tubed defences worn over mail and linking to knee guards, or *poleyns.*

As the need for greater protection increased, it became common, following on from continental fashion, for a horseman to wear additional protection in the form of a poncho-like garment reinforced with steel plates both back and front. Shoulder defenses – *ailettes* – were added, often sporting the wearer's heraldry. Shields, shaped like the base of an iron and curved to conform to the contours of the body, still had their uses. The increasing use of the longbow after 1300 spurred the need for yet further improvements. Mail alone could not resist the deadly bodkin point and gutter-shaped plate defenses to the arms and legs were introduced, strapped on over the hauberk.

For the knight, aside from harness, his biggest single investment was in his war horse or destrier (*dextrarius*), which would be likely to cost around £40, a hefty expense, equal to twice the basic property qualification for knight service. Good bloodstock came from France, Spain and Hungary. These animals were not as large as modern hunters, typically between 15 and 16 hands but with good, strong legs, deep chest and broad back. Generally, the destrier was reserved for the charge, so on the road a knight would ride his everyday palfrey whilst his men jogged along behind on inexpensive *rounceys* (essentially an all-purpose nag).

With its high bow and cantle, the knight's saddle provided good support with additional protection against slashing cuts. Coupled with the use of stirrups, this gave the knight the necessary platform for effective combat. The valuable war horse was also armored to a certain degree, with two sections of protective covering, before and behind the saddle. The front part covered the head with openings for nose, eyes and mouth, the longer rear section reached as far as the hocks. This leather and quilted harness was stiffened by the *chanfron*, a plate section shaped to the horse's face, as that was a common target for the foot soldiers. This fusion of man and horse, both heavily protected, was true armored warfare and the charge was truly frightening.

In terms of its symbolic potency the sword was the very emblem of the gentleman, blades imbued with the legendary lure of Albion and Excalibur. By the early 14th century the knightly sword was a long-bladed, predominantly single handed weapon; double-edged with a broad, straight, full-length fuller (a bevelled groove or slot). Hand and a half swords, "swords of war," or "bastard-swords" sported longer blades. There is a record, from Edward's time, of a sword from Cologne with a blade length of 45 inches (114 cm) and a 5-inch (13 cm) hilt. Quillons were long and either straight or turned up toward the point.

As he prepared himself for combat, the knight would keep his **lance** in the upright position. The lighter spear-like weapon of the Conquest era had given way to a stouter, heavier model that was carried in a couched position under the arm, held securely against the rider's flank and angled to the left over the neck of his mount, resting on the shield. The amount of movement was limited; a wider arc could only be created by "aiming" the horse, but the force would be terrific. When he trotted forward, building to a canter, he'd lift his lance clear of the rest and wedge his behind firmly against the cantle. He'd then lean forward with knees fixed; something like a modern jockey. In this position the shock of impact, which could otherwise result in an ignominious and potentially fatal tumble, was taken mostly by the horse. The position also facilitated using the sword once the lance, essentially a "one-shot" weapon, was thrust.

Heavily-armored 16th-century riders and their barded war horses at the Metropolitan Museum of Art, New York.

Daggers were a preferred accessory, fashioned like miniature swords and intended for stabbing. It was standard practice to dispatch an armored opponent, once brought down, by the point of a knife, driven in through the sights of the helmet, or into an armpit or groin. Infantry might carry the heavy broad-bladed falchion, a cleaver-like weapon, which could deliver a cut of tremendous force. A very fine example of such a sword, the Conyers Falchion, is housed in Durham Cathedral. This is reputed to have been the weapon Sir John Lambton used to kill off the notorious Lambton Worm.

Then, of course, there was the English yeoman with his bow, arguably one of the most effective missile weapons ever developed. One bowman at Agincourt delivered a "kill ratio" not seen again until 1914 (see chapter 5). The bow was not a knight's weapon, though all classes practiced with the bow for war, hunting and sport. Only later, during the 16th century, did the term "longbow" come into use. A plainer expression, "bow"

The late German sallet combination of Emperor Maximilian I.

or "livery bow" was more common during the 15th and before. Retained or liveried archers normally carried their own bows but, in the long drama of the French wars, the Office of Ordnance began issuing standardized kit on campaign to replace those lost or damaged. Large quantities of bows were manufactured to a standard or government pattern, like the infantry musket of following centuries.

Even as full harness was on the brink of obsolescence, the late 15th century witnessed a final, superlative flowering of the armorer's art; fine plate armors that could resist even the deadly "arrow storm." Italian kit of this era was skilfully and beautifully constructed to maximize deflection. Defenses for the vulnerable areas at the shoulder, elbow and knees were strengthened and ribs added to vulnerable areas to deflect killing blows. German craftsmen moved this concept toward the angular perfection of the Gothic style, with its emphasis on uncompromising lines, swept by heavy fluting. A harness of this period might weigh around 60 pounds (30 kg) and would not greatly inhibit the mobility of a robust man, trained since boyhood to move and fight in plate armor.

Italian and German styles came together in Flanders, a flourishing center of manufacture where Italian armorers produced a hybrid style featuring the flexible, fluted plates of the Gothic combined with the more rounded pauldrons (shoulder defenses) and tassets (thigh guards) of their native style. Such armor was sold in large quantities in England, as evidenced by their regular appearance in funerary monuments.

Fifteenth-century plate armor.

For head protection, the stylish sallet form of helmet was popular from the mid-15th century onwards. The rear of the elegantly curved brim swept downwards into a pointed tail to provide extra deflection to the back of the head and neck. Usually provided with a fixed or moveable visor, the sallet was accompanied by the bevor, which afforded protection to the throat and lower face. Although knights could move freely, even in full plate, thirst and heat exhaustion were constant threats even in winter campaigning. "Butcher" Clifford suffered the penalty for unstrapping your bevor in the heat of battle. An opportunist archer shot him down.

At this time the knight's sword reached the apex of its development prior to its eclipse, in the next century, by the rapier. Blades were designed for both cut and thrust. Long and elegantly tapering, with a full grip that could be hefted in one or two hands, in section resembling a flattened diamond; simple quillons, curved or straight, a wheel, pear or kite shaped pommel.

The fight

The armored knight represented shock and awe on the field. Though it's unlikely a mounted charge ever reached the speeds attained by Hollywood knights on film, the sight of these caparisoned horsemen, grimly anonymous in their crested helmets, would be terrifying, particularly to raw infantry. Once tumbled from his horse, however, the knight forfeited his apparent invulnerability. William the Lion, surprised as he besieged Alnwick in 1174, boldly charged his attackers, unhorsing the first one. Then his horse was killed and the knight was hopelessly pinned beneath the carcass.

Once battle was joined, the combat became an intensely personal affair, a hacking, stamping mêlée of bills, spears,

One of the most popular knightly weapons of the 15th century was the fearsome **poleaxe**; a heavy axe blade on a robust ash shaft, some four to six feet in length, a hefty "beak" or hammer head on the reverse of the blade with the head tapering to a wicked spike. This tool was designed to defeat the armorer's art by "opening up" an opponent, a crude but deadly can opener! Popular in the tourney and judicial duel, the blade was secured by steel strips or "languets" intended to prevent lopping off the head. The doomed Duke of Somerset, cornered at the first battle of St. Albans in 1455, fought bravely and decked four Yorkists before a blow from a poleaxe finished him off. Swiss peasants had already proven the worth of their halberds and English bills had contributed to the glorious string of victories in France.

Helmeted Knight of France, illustration by Paul Mercuri in Costumes Historiques *(Paris, 1860–1861).*

German 13th-century great helm.

swords and axes. Men, half blind in armor, soon prone to raging thirst and fatigue, would swiftly become disorientated. Few would be killed by a single blow but a disabling wound, bringing the victim down, would expose him to a fatal, often horrific flurry.

Battle could be divided into a number of phases, commencing latterly with an archery duel. The side that came off worst would be forced to come into contact. Cavalry would then advance and engage with their opposite numbers or, as at Falkirk and Bannockburn, charge (unwisely) into the enemy's spears. When one side broke, the pursuit would be both long and bloody.

The mass grave at Towton

Archaeology, unclouded by layers of rosy romance, occasionally offers us glimpses of what the medieval battlefield was actually like. Several mass graves of the fallen defenders of Visby (1361) were uncovered from 1905 onwards. An enduring question concerning the field of Towton, the bloodiest in English history, has always been: Where are the bodies? The remains of possibly 28,000 combatants would require a significant number of grave-pits to accommodate them. Tradition maintained that, in addition to burials in Saxton Church, pits were dug in "Bloody Meadow" and "the Graves." Tumuli, visible toward the south-west corner of the field, adjacent to the Cock Beck, may constitute inhumation or perhaps more likely date from prehistoric times. A preliminary archaeological investigation, initiated by Towton Battlefield Society in 1993, was inconclusive. Trial trenches, sunk to a depth of 24 inches (61 cm), swiftly became waterlogged and yielded no traces.

A startling new revelation was to come to light much closer to our own times, in July 1996 when building work was underway at Towton Hall. Here, contractors excavating foundations for a proposed garage extension unearthed a shallow pit which contained nearly two dozen skulls. Once it was clear this was not a crime scene the archaeologists took over. That September, digging was extended to reveal the full extent of the inhumation. The burial chamber was some 3.25 meters x 2 meters with a depth of 0.65 meters, and contained the remains of no less than 51 male skeletons who died aged 16–50 years. Aside from a trio of silver rings and other traces, there was no data from which to identify a date for the burial. However, the remains exhibited significant evidence of serious battle-related trauma. These must surely be the forgotten victims of Towton.

Some of the dead, the shortest being 5 feet 2½ inches (158.5 cm), were small men. These were typically from the younger age range. The older men had been taller, with an average height measurement of 5 feet 8 inches (171.6 cm). Most, as far as could be determined, showed little signs of disease, though they'd all done hard physical labor. Dietary traces and dental evidence were consistent, though: these men had neglected their basic dental hygiene.

At least two of the dead, older men, had evidence of previous trauma, suggesting they were seasoned veterans,

A leather jack, like those worn by the Steel Bonnets.

perhaps of the French wars, who had finally met their deaths at the hands of fellow Englishmen. Three exhibited signs of development associated with the practice of archery. Others were less robust and perhaps represented "scraping the barrel" in recruiting terms.

That their deaths were shockingly violent was soon obvious. The Towton mass grave tells a very different story from any of our more stylized and glorious views of medieval warfare. Skull injuries strongly suggest the victims were not wearing protective headgear at the point of death. This gave rise to some initial suggestions that these were revenge killings, cold-blooded murder enacted after the fight. This now appears unlikely. Possibly the fleeing men threw aside their helmets as they ran. Dumping kit and harness to facilitate flight would only be natural. It might be – and this is highly speculative – that some archers fought without steel caps preferring soft hats, steel sallets being a hindrance to the draw.

In medieval conflict head wounds are generally the most commonly identified cause of mortality. Of the 28 skulls that could be successfully examined, 27 had suffered trauma to the head. Interestingly, nine of these had suffered prior and healed damage in the same area. One particularly unlucky individual exhibited no less than nine injuries. In total, 13 had identifiable wounds to the body. Obviously, many more such injuries might have been inflicted without leaving archaeological traces;

abdominal wounds, penetrative strikes entering lungs and general damage to soft tissue would all have occurred. However, there is a general absence of traces of any damage to rib-cages, which may suggest the men had been wearing jacks or harness.

Scoring of bones is suggestive of blades rather than blunter weapons such as the mace or poleaxe. Most prevalent traces were cuts to hands and arms, defensive wounds typically occurring when the victim was attempting to parry or deflect. This would further account for injuries to the left side of the neck and collarbone, inflicted by a right-handed opponent. More wounds to the back of the neck would have occurred while the victim was in flight or already on the ground. The angle of some blows clearly suggests they were inflicted by a mounted assailant. There was nothing pretty about this fight.

One victim's skull was so mangled it required a near-complete reconstruction. He was one of those who'd survived an earlier injury (a depressive fracture to the left parietal region). Death had resulted from a series of eight "penetrating and non-penetrating" wounds, sustained in the course of hand-to-hand combat facing a right-handed attacker swinging a blade, probably a fair-sized weapon, perhaps a hand-and-a-half – or "bastard" – sword. One massive swinging cut to the rear of the skull had inflicted catastrophic and probably fatal, certainly disabling, damage. This was delivered with a "large bladed instrument in a slightly down-to-up motion." In the frenzy of battle a further two blows were added. It is unlikely our victim noticed either of these.

On average, each victim had sustained four wounds. One was dispatched with a single stroke; the unluckiest required 13. Some 65% of the injuries were inflicted by blades, some sheering along the bone, others biting deep or through. Most seem to have been inflicted from the front, suggesting combat rather than rout. Although percussive wounds were less frequent, they were more damaging. Most were delivered against the face or side of the head, smashing blows, crushing bone. Of the total skulls, eight had suffered stabbing wounds, a dozen in all. Delivered to the side or rear of the head these were more surgical in nature, the point of the sword or dagger driven home then twisted free. Sword thrusts were the minority – only three; the others were caused by points or beaks of staff weapons. One unfortunate had been prone when at least two of his three hurts were delivered. The shape of some of the wounds suggested those made either by bodkin pointed arrows or the chunkier penetrations from crossbow bolts.

Forensic anthropologist Shannon A. Novak has suggested that, had these Towton dead been exhumed closer to the epicenter of the fight, then more evidence of arrow wounds would have been detected. The logic of this appears compelling, although we'll have to wait for further discoveries. It is obvious that such a relative handful of remains from so extensive a butcher's bill cannot be said to be wholly representative. It does seem likely that these were victims from the latter stages of the fighting, the rout, who had perhaps cast aside the helmets that might otherwise have given them protection from these awful blows.

Forensic facial reconstruction has provided us with a unique insight into the battle and the men who fought there. One of the faceless dead has been given back his features. An older man, one who had survived previous trauma. Bar the substantial cut across the lower right side of his face, the blow that shattered his jaw, he looks like any typical blunt faced artisan. This treatment of a prior injury hints at a level of battlefield surgery both sophisticated and competent. Such evidence and his strong physique suggest a seasoned bowman, one who might have seen much action. Like his comrades in the pit his luck clearly ran out at Towton where he sustained eight frenzied blows to the head. This skilled and fascinating process has given us something we have not had before, the face of an actual combatant. Not the stylized portraiture or imagery of kings or magnates but the no-nonsense face of the ordinary footslogger.

Of all the knights who ever broke a lance, William the Marshal, Earl of Pembroke (1147–1219) was probably nearest to an Arthurian ideal. He came from a rough neighborhood, and his father, John, supported Matilda during the Anarchy (the civil war waged between her and King Stephen from 1135–1154). Young William had been handed to the king as a hostage when he besieged Newbury Castle in 1152, and shortly thereafter was sent off to the household of a relative, William de Tankerville, to learn the chivalric arts. Marshal was a quick learner and showed great promise. He was both blooded and knighted on campaign in Upper Normandy in 1166. Though knighthood was the vocation of gentlemen and war their preferred medium, honor and glory were always subordinate to profit. A year later young William contended in his first tournament. Here he found his true vocation: Not only was he very good, he also made a handsome profit.

For a short while, William served his maternal uncle Patrick, Earl of Salisbury, until the earl was killed in ambush and William was captured, suffering a nasty thigh wound that could easily have proved fatal. He was eventually ransomed by Eleanor of Aquitaine herself, who'd heard of his prowess. He then became a professional jouster – the Premier League footballer of his day – amassing celebrity and wealth as he went. He later claimed he'd defeated 500 knights in the lists. These early tournaments (as Scott portrays in *Ivanhoe*) tended to be lively; there wasn't much of a rule book and fatalities were common.

He entered service with the aging Henry II, and the king was well pleased with his protégée. Rewards followed and William dutifully supported Henry when his son Richard rebelled and allied himself to Philip II of France. In one skirmish, he unhorsed the Lionheart himself: there weren't many who could achieve that. William spared his captive injury, and to give Richard his due he never bore a grudge and following his subsequent victory allowed William to go through with his proposed marriage to

Isabel de Clare (he was 43, she 17). Her dowry was generous, though William didn't finally get his hands on the earldom of Pembroke till 1199. He'd gone from landless younger son to leading nobleman within a few years, and lavished much of his wife's cash on improving both Pembroke and Chepstow castles.

When Richard left for his cherished, if foolish, foray into crusading, William was left behind as a member of the regency council. He soon fell out with Prince John, though William's eldest brother died fighting for Lackland. Richard awarded William the Marshal's baton his disloyal sibling had held. Despite their differences, William supported John's kingship on Richard's death, but even William's military skills couldn't save John's position in Normandy and they fell out once again. The Marshal had a significant personal stake in Normandy that he wasn't keen to wave goodbye to, and negotiated separately with French King Philip II on his own account. To accomplish this, he had to bend his knee to Philip. John was not best pleased, and the rift between them deepened. John was spiteful and vindictive; William was pushed out and humiliated.

The Marshal spent some time in Ireland until he and the king were reconciled in 1212. John needed whatever friends he could find and William, despite all the provocations, had remained loyal. He stayed with the king through the First Barons' War and it was to William that the dying John entrusted the future of his son and his crown. William's loyalty never wavered; he won the Second Battle of Lincoln and saved young Henry's throne. His policy of reconciliation and fairness went a long way to healing the divide. Even when, in 1219, his health began to fail he managed to effect a workable settlement that left young Henry secure. He died on May 14, 1219 and is buried in Temple Church, London.

TIMELINE

1095	Battle of Hastings – William kills Harold
1095	Pope Urban calls for the First Crusade
1099	Capture of Jerusalem – the Kingdom of Heaven is proclaimed
1106	Battle of Tinchebrai – Henry I wins the Battle for Normandy
1119/1129	Knightly Orders formed
1138	Battle of the Standard – the Scots are seen off by the northern lords
1147	Battle of Doryleum – the Crusaders are defeated
1187	Siege and fall of Jerusalem
1191/1192	Siege of Acre – Lionheart defeats Saladin, massacres garrison
1204	Crusaders take Byzantium – a brief Latin kingdom in the east
1213	Battle of Muret – De Montfort the Elder's greatest victory
1264	Battle of Lewes – Henry III defeated by de Montfort
1265	Battle of Evesham – de Montfort defeated by Longshanks
1277/1283	Edwardian conquest of Wales
1304	Battle of Courtrai – burghers take on and defeat mounted knights
1314	Battle of Bannockburn – the Scots defeat the English
1340	Battle of Sluys – a sea battle and famous English victory

1346 Battle of Crecy – Edward III defeats the French

1348 Edward III founds the Order of the Knights of the Garter

1356 Battle of Poitiers – The Black Prince's famous victory

1415 Battle of Agincourt – the arrow storm again defeats the French

1429 Siege of Orleans – Joan of Arc comes to the rescue

1453 Battle of Castillon – the English are finally defeated in France Siege and fall of Byzantium – End of the old Eastern Empire

1455 First Battle of St. Albans – the wars of the Roses kick off; Yorkist victory

1471 Battle of Barnet – the "Kingmaker" meets his end

1485 Battle of Bosworth – the death of Richard III

1513 Siege of Norham – artillery decides the day

1522 Battle of Biocca – massed musketry defeats pikes

CHAPTER 1

1066 AND ALL THAT

I'll tell of the Battle of Hastings,
As happened in days long gone by,
When Duke William became King of England,
And 'Arold got shot in the eye.
Marriott Edgar

AFTERNOON ON OCTOBER 14, 1066, AUTUMN in the garden of England. The battle had lasted all day and it wasn't over yet. The stubborn shield wall was holding despite constant battering from Norman infantry and cavalry. Less than a month before, the last great clash of the Viking Age had occurred far to the north at Stamford Bridge, east of York. Harald Hardrada and King Harold of England's renegade brother Tostig faced the last English king and his elite *huscarls*. The Norse invaders were cut to pieces; Hardrada died a true Viking, sword in hand.

Now King Harold faced a different enemy: not just a new opponent but a different set of tactics. The cream of Duke William's army was comprised of mounted knights, warriors on horseback. It was a new fashion but for hours the old shield wall had still pushed them back. Dusk wasn't far off. Harold just had to hang on. A commando of knights has forced its way onto the plateau – most won't be coming back but at least four get through and kill Harold. The last Saxon King may or may not have been shot in the eye, but he's still dead and his body horribly mutilated. As his banner dipped and fell, so did Saxon England. It was a whole new era – the Age of Chivalry.

Origins of knighthood

Detail from the Bayeux Tapestry showing William the Conqueror (center), his half-brothers Robert, Count of Mortain (right) and Odo, Bishop of Bayeux in the Duchy of Normandy (left).

What made a knight? Origins are lost in history but it may have been Charlemagne who, fearful of Danish raiders – *ruffians*, as he called them – appointed key local men to defend their communities. Now Charlemagne was a Christian and it was his rather heavy-handed conversion tactics that had irritated the pagan Danes. But at the outset there was no direct link between knighthood and the church. That came later. When Pope Urban called for a great crusade to free the Holy Land in 1095, he may have had it in mind to provide job opportunities for unemployed knights who were otherwise a menace at home. He made it official, taking the cross became a badge of respectability, and the initiate had to promise he would

> defend to the uttermost the oppressed, the widow and the orphan, and that women of noble birth should enjoy his special care.

This really was the birth of chivalry – the notion that a knight was more than a bruiser, a professional fighter; he represented an ideal of service and honor.

This new connection between church and knight, between faith and the sword, meant that being a knight put you into a special category. The ideals of chivalry were what defined you, and knighthood was a status that had to be earned rather than one automatically conferred by birth. The poorest gentleman from the shires, any rustic D'Artagnan, was likely to be as good a knight as anyone from higher up the ladder. Becoming a knight involved a religious passage akin to secular ordination, and this was carried further by the knightly orders which grew from the crusades (see Chapter 2).

As we've seen from the glittering career of William Marshal, the tournament was both an industry and an obsession. One stage removed from gladiatorial combat, this was a hugely popular spectator sport: the bloodier, the better. Tournaments were the Rotary Clubs of their day, an international freemasonry of knights who by breeding, status and training were elevated way above the lumpen masses. But the highly stylized jousts of the Tudor age were a long way in the future, as at this time tournaments were rough and ready, a free-for-all where injuries and death were by no means rare.

In 1274 King Edward I was invited by the Count of Chalons to take part in a tournament. Hundreds were involved on each side and the fracas became known as the Little Battle of Chalons. The count tried every trick he knew to throw Edward from his saddle, but the king was too quick for him and it was the count who ended up in the dust. Thoroughly humiliated, he re-mounted and attacked Edward full-on. His French followers joined in with gusto. As did the English archers who let fly and shot many of their hosts. Dozens died, and yet it wasn't until the next century that rules were instated. The safety fence separating combatants – the tilt – wasn't introduced until 1420.

The Homeric ideal of single combat translated easily from joust to battlefield. Robert the Bruce won a significant victory when, on June 23, 1314, the first day of Bannockburn, despite only being lightly armored, he brained Sir Henry de Bohun, an English knight who came at him in full kit. Earlier, William Wallace ("Braveheart") and Bishop Bek had slogged it out in the streets of Glasgow. Before he fought the Count of Chalons,

Sixteenth-century German print, showing Henry II of France jousting.

Edward had won the Second Barons' War. In the Forest of Alton, in what may have been a confused skirmish, the rebel knight Adam Gurdon, a leading local rebel had clashed with Edward in single combat. Gurdon was a tough fighter with something of a reputation and the duel was long and hard-fought. Edward won but was prepared to show mercy to a worthy adversary and spared Gurdon.

An Englishman's castle

The knightly warrior was defined by his status, by his membership of the feudal elite, distinguished by his armor, his weapons and his warhorse. Moreover, he was identified by his castle. Prior to 1066, these were rare in England. Thereafter, they proliferated. Not merely a fort or a refuge, the castle was the dominion of the feudal gentry writ in solid masonry.

Castles live in the mind, the visible traces of the age of knighthood. Castell Coch in South Wales and fantastical Neuschwanstein in Bavaria (a fairy-tale confection commissioned by King Ludwig

Statue of William Wallace, Aberdeen.

II) were both built as 19th century homage to the ideal. Arundel, Alnwick, Bamburgh, Edinburgh, Framlingham, Stirling, Windsor: Britain is studded with castles from vast royal palaces to lonely towers such as Smailholm, Gilnockie or Neidpath. Castles dominate our literature of chivalry from Malory to Bernard Cornwell and, let's face it – we'd all like one; cold draughty, damp and uncomfortable as they mostly are.

Warfare was, for four centuries after the Norman Conquest, dominated by the perpetual and symbiotic duel between those who built castle walls and those who tried to knock them down. This contest continued until the age of gunpowder profoundly altered the balance. Prior to that, the advantage typically lay with the defender. It is widely believed that it was the Normans, with their timber motte-and-bailey fortifications, who introduced the archetypal castle into England, though some historians now dispute this. During the 12th century, timber was gradually replaced by masonry; great stone keeps such as Rochester, Orford, Conisburgh, Richmond and Newcastle, soared impressively.

The castle was not just a fort; it was the knight's residence the seat and symbol of his power, the center of his administration, and a secure base from which his mailed household could hold down a swathe of territory. Castles were both practical and symbolic. The civil wars between Stephen and Mathilda (also known as the Anarchy) spawned a rash of unlicensed building, fuelling the noble threat to crown authority. Castles grew thickest on the disputed marches of England, facing Welshmen and Scots; in the north-west, the mighty red sandstone fortress of Carlisle stood firm, often attacked, never taken; a clear statement to the Scots.

Concentric castles, influenced by Arab and Byzantine models, appeared when Edward I began building his great chain of towering Welsh fortresses. As the country had enjoyed a long spell of peace before that, many lords had invested in what might now be termed "makeovers" – aiming to improve standards of living rather than add to defenses. Larger, more ornate chapels and great halls replaced their workaday predecessors; gardens and orchards were laid out to provide tranquil spaces within the complex.

Cross given by Mathilda, Abbess of Essen (973–1011), typical of medieval devotion.

Most castles of the earlier period relied upon the strength of the great keep: towering in fine ashlar with the lower vaulted basement reserved for storage and an entrance at first floor level, frequently later enclosed in a defensive fore-building. On this level, we would typically find the great hall with a chapel and the lord's private apartment – or "solar" – on the second floor above. Spiral stairs were set in the thickness of the wall leading to a rooftop parapet walk, often with corner towers. The keep – or "donjon" – was surrounded by a strong stone wall enclosing the courtyard or bailey which would also house the usual domestic offices. The keep was essentially a refuge, a passive defense.

From the reign of Henry II onward, strong flanking towers were frequently added to provide defense against mining. The isolated polygonal keep at Orford in Suffolk (1165–1173) is a fine example of this. At Pembroke, William Marshal built an entirely circular keep. The curtain wall was also raised and strengthened, complete with D-shaped towers, the section lying beyond the curtain wall rounded at the corners to frustrate mining. These towers made the attacker's job far more difficult. If he breached or surmounted, a section of the rampart, he would be corralled between the towers that would, now and in turn, have to be assaulted separately. This

Detail from the Morgan Bible, 13th century.

Traditional timber engines like the **ballista** and the **mangonel** dominated siege warfare during the 13th century. The ballista was, in effect, a giant crossbow that hurled a bolt or occasionally stones at the enemy's walls. It was intended as an anti-personnel weapon, smacking unwary defenders from the parapet, used to cover an assault or "escalade."

Reconstructed Trebuchet at Middelaldercentret, Denmark.

The **trebuchet**, most likely Arabic in origin, worked by counterpoise. The weapon was built with a central timber beam pivoting between two sturdy posts; one end of the beam had ropes affixed and the sling was fitted to the other. Initially, when the ball was loaded into the sling, a group of hefty squaddies simply hauled on the ropes, pivoting upwards the shorter end of the timber, to ensure the sling, at just the right moment, released the projectile. Latterly the men were replaced by a timber-framed box casing filled with rubble. By now these machines were much larger and the box might weight anything over 10,000 pounds (4,536 kg).

was leading toward the concentric design where the strength of the fortress was distributed through the towers and the great keep, as a principal feature, became far less important.

Siege

When the knight or castellan became aware that a siege was imminent, it was time to prepare. Clearly, adequate foodstuffs and a clean water supply were essential to maintain the garrison for what might stretch to several months of encirclement. Livestock would be gathered in, and the surrounding countryside stripped to deny the attackers. Ditches would be cleared and consolidated; repairs to the masonry undertaken, trees, bushes and inconvenient settlements would be demolished to deny cover to the enemy. Timber hoardings – called "brattices" – would be erected over the parapet walk to provide a covered fighting platform. The defenders' own artillery was serviced, repaired as necessary, and supplies of missiles and arrows brought in.

Siege warfare was costly, time-consuming and tedious. The attacker might be stuck before the defenses for several long and frustrating weeks, gobbling up his supplies at a fearsome rate, at risk from the defenders' sallies, from dysentery in the crowded, insanitary trenches or from the arrival of a relief force. He would try to negotiate, to persuade the castellan to come to terms. If the latter acceded before the lines were fixed, convention would allow the defenders to march out under arms and depart unmolested.

If cajolery failed, then threats might suffice. Captives were handy pawns. In 1139 King Stephen persuaded the mother of Roger le Poer to surrender Devizes or see her son hanged before the walls. Edward III, in 1333, before the walls of Berwick, threatened to hang the governor's two young sons if the gates remained closed. The latter refused and had to endure the agony of watching the wretched youths die. Edward, like his grandfather, didn't issue idle threats.

If a siege dragged on, any inclination to mercy shrank. Should the place fall to storm then the attacker could put all within to the sword. Where the defenders, finding themselves in dire straits, subsequently sued for terms, they might find the besieger less amenable than at the outset. Even when a commander was disposed to magnanimity, his soldiers, deprived of loot, might be disinclined to take heed. Edward I, who'd let his men run riot in the streets of Berwick in 1296 was finally so appalled he called a halt and you couldn't ever call him squeamish. Civil wars were worse. Kings and magnates would not normally wish to see towns sacked unless, as in the case of the notorious siege and storming of Beziers in July 1209 during the suppression of the Cathars, the whiff of heresy was about. The French knights, breaking in, slaughtered everyone, heretics and believers alike. The Papal legate Arnaud Almaric reportedly said:

Kill them all. God will know his own.

Morale was ever, vital. A loss of nerve on the besiegers' part could lead to failure. The effects of exhaustion and hunger could swiftly erode a garrison's will to resist. When laying siege to Stirling in 1304, Edward I refused to allow the defenders to formally surrender. The king had got his engineers to build a giant trebuchet, the "War Wolf" and he was anxious to test its effect. Henry V, in the 15th century, refused to allow French civilians, expelled by the garrison commanders as *bouches inutiles* ("useless mouths"), to pass through the lines. They stayed trapped in no-man's-land, left to squat in filth and famine while the siege continued. Disease was a specter that stalked both sides, especially during hot summer weather, yet it was extremely difficult to maintain a siege during stark and freezing winter.

Starving the defenders entailed less tactical risk than attacking, but was time-consuming and expensive. The besieger had to plan and fortify his camp, proof his trenches against sallies, stockpile supplies, provide tents or bothies for his men and attempt some basic form of temporary sanitation. To be effective, the blockade had to seal off the besieged completely from re-supply. When throwing his great ring of concentric castles around the conquered principality of Wales, Edward sited these so that, in the main, they could be re-supplied from the sea. If the defenders could receive fresh supplies then the besieger's task was made almost impossible.

Any full-scale siege was likely to be a long term and static affair, tying down the attacker's army and robbing him of any strategic initiative. The alternative – bypassing the castle and leaving a hostile behind you – was equally unappealing. As a compromise, the attackers could leave a sufficient number of men to neutralize the castle while the bulk of the attacking force remained active in the field.

Frightfulness, what we'd now call terror, was another tactic available to the attacker. He could frighten the besieged into surrendering by wreaking havoc on his surrounding lands. In 1123 Henry I "took up" all the space around Pont-Audemer for a good 20 miles or so. Contemporary writers confirm that the army's scouts or prickers acted as incendiaries and foragers, seizing what they might use, destroying the rest. Again, these tactics were limited during civil strife.

Where the attacking general had decided to make an attempt on walls, he'd send in his assault troops, who would attempt to set ladders. Archers, protected by timber hoardings ("pavises"), would unleash a missile storm intended to keep the defenders' heads down. For their part the castellan's men would rely on their own bows and on a range of projectiles to smash the ladders, bunching reserves to take on whoever got onto the parapet, desperate and bloody. If the castle was protected by a strong water defense that frustrated attempts at mining, the attacker might go for the base of the walls with a ram or screw, maneuvered over the moat after a pontoon of fascines (bundles of sticks) had been laid.

This ram would be a solid baulk of timber housed in a wheeled shed, offering the crew some protection. The beam was slung on ropes from the roof, swung to and fro to gather momentum. A screw was used to bore rather than batter. Defenders would lower large hooks to catch and fling aside or drop great boulders to smash the protective lid and crush its occupants. The "belfry" was a movable timber tower, higher at its upper level than the wall and providing a platform for archers while infantry charged across a drawbridge. Like all big wooden structures these monsters were difficult to move, vulnerable to fire and involved a great deal of effort in their construction.

Mining had an ancient provenance; Joshua used it before the great walls of Jericho. For the miner, it was difficult and dangerous. A shaft was sunk from a distance to extend under a corner of the great tower, with a chamber excavated directly underneath. This was supported by timber props, crammed with combustible material and then fired to collapse a section of wall. Naturally architects would attempt to frustrate the miners' efforts by siting the castle on a foundation of solid rock or by creating water defenses. Furthermore, the base of the wall could be splayed or "battered" to provide an even more solid obstacle. The miner had to conceal the entry to his shaft to avoid alerting the defenders.

We can't think of knights without imagining **castles** and the two are completely entwined. We're lucky that, even today, so many medieval strongholds survive; many were renovated in the UK in the 19th century. In the county of Northumberland, the castles Alnwick, Bamburgh and Lindisfarne were "restored" as comfortable country houses for wealthy urbanites, as were many others. Some, such as Bodiam or Herstmonceaux, were built late and, while they look like forts, were really houses. If you want to feel what it was really like for our medieval soldiers, forget baronial Gothic and go to Hermitage, the grim uncompromising "strength" of far-off Liddesdale, a place whose history is as grim as it looks.

Dead ground or buildings could provide ideal cover. As an alternative to bringing down a section of wall, the shaft could continue into the bailey, like the reverse of an escape tunnel.

A prudent castellan might place buckets of water on his ramparts to detect tremors. If the wall was breached then the defenders would attempt to plug the gap with timbers or construct temporary screen walls. The more enterprising, on detecting mining against the walls, might attempt to sink a countermine. The object was to break into the attackers' shaft and engage the miners in a desperate and savage subterranean mêlée. Readers of Sebastian Faulks's highly accomplished Great War novel *Birdsong* will recall how these tactics were still employed on the Western Front.

►─── Profile: Sir Henry Percy ───◄

Whereat the great lord of Northumberland,
Whose warlike ears could never brook retreat,
Cheer'd up the drooping army

Shakespeare *Henry VI Part 3*, 1:1

In Alnwick, not far from the castle, there's a great bronze statue of Sir Henry Percy, better known as "Hotspur" (1364–1403). If you miss that one, don't worry – there's another inside. Of Norman stock, the Percy family (all, helpfully, named Henry) mostly had estates in Yorkshire until they bought the Barony of Alnwick from Bishop Bek, a slippery prelate (the sale was possibly fraudulent). This was early in the 14th century, when the Scottish wars were beginning to bite. The Northumbrian gentry were ruined by the escalating costs of homeland defense. This was good for the Percies, who distinguished themselves against the Scots. They gained the coveted post of border warden – a license to raise private armies and gobble up bankrupt estates at fire sale prices. By the time Hotspur's father was created First Earl of Northumberland, they owned a vast acreage. The young Henry was knighted by Richard II and went on to be governor both of Berwick and then of Calais. Hotspur was renowned for his dash and aggression, though nowadays we might call it thuggery. Then again, he lived in very thuggish times.

In August 1388, Hotspur led a northern army against the Scottish Earl of March and James, Earl of Douglas, who had rampaged down the east coast as far as Durham. Legend has it Douglas and Percy had scrapped in front of the wooden barricades at Newcastle, where the Scot stole Hotspur's pennon. March's brigade was only a diversion; the main thrust was to come through the west. He retreated north, torching Ponteland until he got as far as Otterburn where he laid siege to the Umfraville castle there. Percy pushed his men on a long hot day's march and ride until, on the evening of August 19, they caught up with the Scots. Hotspur had the element of surprise but opted for a risky night attack rather than wait for light. This is fraught at the best of times, and the plan went adrift when Umfraville's battalion, trying to feel around the flank, got lost instead.

March was a first-rate commander and a flanking charge led by Douglas finally beat the English, though the earl himself was killed. Hotspur and his brother Ralph were taken prisoner. Percy had to wait 14 years to get his revenge but his turn came on September 14, 1402 at Homildon Hill. Between times, however, his father had conspired against King Richard in favor of Henry Bolingbroke and facilitated his successful coup. Richard was a rather a poor king, to be fair, but kings don't like kingmakers and Henry IV was wary of the Percies; the Earl was the epitome of the "over-mighty subject."

Meanwhile, a new Earl of Douglas led a very large Scots army into Northumberland. Hotspur employed the Earl of March – who'd defected – as his chief of staff and listened to his advice. The English confronted the invaders at Homildon near Wooler. March didn't engage, preferring to use his archers to decimate the enemy ranks. Thousands died and the earl was captured. Homildon was a great victory and Hotspur's star shone in the firmament — but not for long. A dispute over the division of ransoms led to a break with the crown and the Percies were soon talking to Glendower and the Welsh rebels.

On July 21, 1403, Hotspur led a rebel army out at Shrewsbury to face the king's forces. This time, March was fighting for Henry IV, and the battle began with the first longbow duel in English history. It was both bloody and decisive. Hotspur was shot down by an arrow and killed. His duplicitous father lasted another five years before he too died a traitor's death. Thanks to his heroic portrayal in Shakespeare's *Henry IV*, Hotspur has been remembered somewhat more favorably than he probably deserved.

CHAPTER 2

KINGDOM OF HEAVEN

Richard the Lionheart wrote a page in England's book of fame,
History will long recall his name.
Rode like the wind on a pure white stallion,
Leading the way for his crack battalion,
Humble in spite of his victory in York.
Loved by the people he protected,
Blessed in the churches he erected,
In those days of yore.
Lyrics for the theme tune of 1960s ITV
children's series *Richard the Lionheart*

IN THE SUMMER OF 1095, PEASANTS toiling in the fields, their drab monochrome and all too often uncertain lives stretching out in drudgery, would have been astonished and electrified to see the Pope himself, Urban II, touring Christendom to promote his big idea – the Crusades.

Fifteenth-century miniature depicting the conquest of Constantinople in 1204.

The concept wasn't altogether novel. Emperor Michael VII of Byzantium, the rump of the Eastern Empire, had approached Gregory VII begging for assistance against the encroaching Turks. This was music to his Holiness's ears. Gregory had three aims: he wanted to end the schism with the Eastern Church, to unite western Christendom and recover the Holy Places. The price for any aid offered to Byzantium would be re-unification under Rome's roof. Besides, a crusade would offer employment for restless knights and ensure their swords were put to good use in God's work.

Islam had become widespread across Palestine, all along the Maghreb, over the Straits of Gibraltar, into Spain and France. Charles Martel could be described as the first crusader when he halted the tide flowing up the Rhone Valley. The long fight back in Spain had begun, and the legendary Rodrigo diaz de Vivar – "el Cid" – remains one of the most famous knights of all. The Genoese and Pisans had already cleared Muslims from Sardinia while Norman freebooters, grabbing a toehold in Italy, would soon do the same in Sicily.

Many of those who volunteered to "take the cross" were motivated by **religious piety**. Others were more pragmatic. This was an opportunity for restless knights and landless younger sons to carve out kingdoms and reap a harvest of shining loot for themselves – and if the Pope gave the expedition his blessing, all was thought to be holy. News of the crusade was spread by a network of preachers; Urban himself proved tireless. For merchants and traders, it provided a business opportunity; crusaders would need kit and provisions, and also credit. Crusading was going to be expensive and great feudal lords, while asset rich, were often cash-poor.

These Italians weren't necessarily motivated by faith, but by mercantilism. Their prosperity was built on the passage of goods from east to west and vice-versa. Venice was a major commercial player, too. Though Islam had dominated the Levant for centuries, Christian pilgrims had swarmed over the Holy Places, Western Europe's first exercise in mass tourism. When travellers reached fabled Byzantium, they were awed by the scale and splendor of this vast, thriving metropolis – a city of fable, gateway to Asia and the final repository of classical civilization. In due course, it became rather too attractive and the hired guns of the 4th Crusade took the place by storm in 1204.

Byzantium had been militarily formidable but had not recovered from the catastrophe of Lake Manzikert in 1071. Its armed forces, strong enough on paper, were primarily made up of mercenaries. Harald Hardrada – yes, that one – had led the Emperor's elite Varangian Guard, amassing a tidy fortune in the process. Pilgrims were good for business; they thronged the Italian ports, accepting the many dangers that lay in store. Now a harsher regime was barring the tourist sites and Pope Urban had promised Holy War.

Whether Christendom had been seeking such a vast and noble undertaking is hard to judge, but the soil was fertile and the chivalry of Western Europe responded. Nobody had actually planned a viable strategy for recovering the Holy Land. It wasn't going to be easy: distances were enormous and 11th century armies had no real experience of maintaining logistical chains over mountain, steppe and desert. The enemy was formidable and fighting in his own back yard. He was numerically strong, naturally acclimatized to the heat and in possession of strong walled bases.

Hierarchy

Knights did not like serving under other knights, and no supreme commander emerged. Instead, each contingent chose its own leader. Robert Curthose, Godfrey of Bouillon, the

Count of Vermandois, Robert II of Flanders and Raymond, Count of Toulouse were joined as commanders by the dashing (if disreputable) Robert Bohemond, self-styled prince of Taranto. A bit of a ruffian, Bohemond had fought against the Emperor Alexios I Komnenos and trounced his army at the Battle of Dyrrhachium (now Durres in Albania) in 1081.

Crusaders were obliged to bend their knees to the Byzantine Emperor and recover such territory as they might win back in his name. This wasn't really what the knights themselves had in mind,

Before he died, Godfrey had taken steps to create some viable organizational infrastructure in the east, out of which were born the knightly orders – **Templars** and **Hospitallers**. These became the core of the crusaders' military hierarchy. St. Bernard himself was one of those who helped established the Templar order:

> They live with one another happily and with modesty without wenches or children in order that they do not lack evangelical perfection, without property in one house, of one spirit...

Individual knights of the orders are often portrayed as poor warrior monks, living in pious austerity. However, the orders themselves amassed enormous wealth, the Templars managing a nice line in profitable lending and building up vast estates. So rich were they that they finally fell foul of the King of France, who savagely repressed the order.

though they needed both the assistance and tactical expertise of the Byzantines. Only Godfrey acquiesced. Bohemond and his equally aggressive cousin Tancred had their own clearly formed agendas, but they too needed help understanding terrain and fighting Arab armies. The dangerously idealistic Peter the Hermit was leading a parallel "People's Crusade," a disorganized group of knights and peasants who'd blundered across the Bosphorus in search of easy pickings. Instead they found death or enslavement. Peter's disorganized army was slaughtered with contemptuous ease.

This turn of events actually helped the real crusaders, as their opponent, Alp Arslan, decided that if this was the best Christ had to offer, there was no need to get worried. Bohemond led a crusader vanguard that took on crowds of horse archers and held them off long enough for the main force to swing into action and win a stunning victory.

Desert warfare

The crusaders' next target was the city of Nicaea, which fell after a short siege. Antioch proved a far tougher nut and even once taken, turned into a trap when a massive relief force threatened. Peter the Hermit, who'd escaped from the catastrophe he'd created, came up trumps by "finding" a section of the True Cross. This inspired the crusaders, who scattered their enemy, though Bohemond stayed put in Antioch for some time thereafter. It wasn't until January 1099 that the survivors headed off for Jerusalem. Godfrey's younger brother Raymond went off eastwards, ostensibly to shadow the army's flanks, but in fact to find a kingdom of his own.

The march through bare desert had been awful, especially as their adversaries made sure there were no natural resources left available for the westerners. Men and horses died in droves but eventually reached Jerusalem. They swept the city like a

Crac des Chevaliers, Syria, one of the best-preserved Crusader castles.

sandstorm in a riotous display of murder and theft. The Kingdom of Heaven had arrived, the holy cross balanced on mounds of civilian corpses.

Unity was never a crusader characteristic and many returned to the west following the taking of Jerusalem. Godfrey took the throne of Jerusalem but died of fever within the year. Egypt had sent a substantial force to re-take the Holy City but the crusaders beat them soundly at Ascalon that August. The mounted charge of knights proved almost invincible, winning fight after fight.

Next, the crusaders captured the vital port of Jaffa. This was probably the high-water mark – of the Crusades. Holding the inland city of Jerusalem was only viable with a safe route to the coast and re-supply. For nearly half a century, they hung on. Not until a Turkish resurgence in 1144 led to the fall of Edessa did Jerusalem appear in any way threatened. This was a serious setback, leading St Bernard to preach another crusade to shore up these kingdoms beyond the sea – *Outremer*.

Outremer

Both Conrad III of Germany and Louis VII of France led reinforcements to Palestine, though not without great difficulties. They teamed up with Baldwin III of Jerusalem and the Grand Masters of the knightly orders. They aimed to take Damascus with a powerful army. Numbers are always highly speculative but they may have led over 1,000 knights with several thousand supporting troops. The expedition proved a farce – none of the leaders could agree who should keep the city, assuming they managed to take it in the first place. After a collective sulk and with a big Turkish army approaching, they gave up and returned whence they had come.

It wasn't just the crusaders who were incapable of unity; as long as the Turks were split, *Outremer* (the name given to the Crusader states in the Near East) could hang on. One of those who marched to the relief of Damascus was a young man named Saladin. He would achieve what no Muslim leader since Mohammed had managed, and his ascendancy sounded the long death knell of the crusader kingdoms. His life's work would be to recover what had been lost. By 1169 he held Egypt and was eyeing up Palestine. Jerusalem had a clear supply route to the coast and her open landward flank was guarded by a chain of mighty fortresses. In the north, the Byzantines still had enough clout to threaten Syria so Saladin was unlikely to recruit many warriors there.

In September 1176, Saladin's forces defeated Emperor Manuel. This was as big a disaster for the crusaders; with Byzantium in retreat the right man could unite Islam. Saladin was that man. When Manuel died four years later, the die was cast. Saladin now burst out of Egypt, aiming a thrust at Jerusalem, but he'd miscalculated and was seen off by King Baldwin ("the Leper King"). This phase of the struggle ended in a truce and commercial arrangements with free passage for both sides' traders.

Reynald of Chatillon, Prince of Antioch from 1153 to 1160/61, is often portrayed as a villain. The rogue was also a fool. He attacked the Muslim caravans, motivated either by plain greed or the desire to spark a war. If the latter, it worked. In September 1183, Saladin led a retaliatory sweep, bottling the crusader knights in their fortresses. Another truce was patched up and again it was fractured by Reynald. Guy of Lusignan, successor of Baldwin, mobilized his forces and set out seeking battle. It

Miniature from Jean Froissart's Chronicles, depicting the battle of Montiel.

was said the Bishop of Acre accompanied the crusader army who carried sections of the True Cross. Potent as such a talisman should have been, it was no match for Guy's incompetence. Saladin was leading them towards the Sea of Galilee, and tormented by heat, thirst and exhaustion, the exhausted knights camped at the Horns of Hattin, a narrow pass.

To add to their rapidly escalating difficulties, Saladin's men set the sparse, dry grasses alight, smoke concealing his skirmishers who loosed volleys of arrows. The knights couldn't get to grips, even as the contest moved into a second day. The army of heaven began to fracture. Guy lacked the skills to fight such a wily enemy. The knights charged time and time again, but they were in such poor condition many died from exhaustion rather than at the hands of the enemy. It was a *Gotterdammerung* from which the crusaders never recovered. Guy was captured and Reynald put to death. The defeat sealed the fate of Jerusalem,

Tomb of Henry and Eleanor in Fontevrault Abbey, Pays de la Loire, France.

which was surrendered by Balian of Ibelin on October 2, 1187. The crescent had replaced the cross and it wouldn't be shifting.

In Europe, there was horror and mourning. The Pope of the day died of shock (or so it's said), and his replacement, Gregory VIII, immediately issued the call for a fresh attempt to recover Jerusalem, promising the forgiveness of sins and a sure path to heaven for those who died doing God's work. Two months later, he followed his predecessor to the grave, still trying to heal the rift between the fractious Pisans and Genoese.

Henry II of England and Philip Augustus of France were also far from friendly. At home, too, Henry had plenty of domestic problems with his sons, Richard and John. Richard – the Lionheart, of course – has had a mixed press throughout history. Though he was a magnificent warrior and gifted tactician, he could also be capricious and cruel. Nevertheless, the "Lionheart" would become the most famous crusader of all, a superb soldier and knight if, at best, an indifferent king.

Barbarossa

Another key player was the German Emperor Frederick Barbarossa. In his late sixties, old by the standards of the day and a highly successful monarch for decades, he'd already subdued his enemies at home and was up for a crack at the Middle East. He thoroughly prepared the ground and even entered into polite (if pointless) correspondence with Saladin. On May 11, 1189, the German contingent marched out. It was a sizeable, well-disciplined army, and its passage through Hungary went well. Once into Byzantine territory, however, they were soon scrapping with Serbian bandits. The Emperor panicked and jailed Frederick's messengers. Soon, the Germans were getting ready to besiege Byzantium, which panicked the Emperor still further and persuaded him to offer terms.

Keeping his men well in hand, Barbarossa crossed into Asia. He soon found any agreements with local rulers were totally useless, as his forces suffered increasing attacks that culminated in a pitched battle at Iconium (present-day Konya). Here, the Germans scored a great victory. So far so good, but in early June, the ageing Emperor died as he was crossing a river. Whether he just fell and was drowned or whether he suffered a heart attack or stroke is unclear. He was gone, and his crusade died with him. The army disintegrated and Saladin gave thanks to God.

England and France

By now Henry II was also dead and Richard, at 32, was king. He and Philip Augustus, eight years his younger, had patched up their differences to take the cross. Physically the English king resembled a new Achilles – handsome, brave, with a superb physique and an ability to charm. Much of this was superficial. Philip Augustus, if less prepossessing, was sharper and more inclined to *realpolitik*. Both went crusading at the same time as neither would trust the other if left at home. Richard's Angevin inheritance included much of France, most of which Philip Augustus wanted back.

Travelling by different routes, the two armies were to rendezvous in Sicily. Richard's sister Joanna had been married to the previous king of the island, but he had been succeeded by his cousin Tancred, who treated Joanna very badly. Sicily was not a success. The French behaved well enough but Richard's Englishmen scrapped with the locals while he fumed over the insult to his family. Matters went from bad to worse, riots and confrontations followed until Richard, allowing his temper to get the better of him, launched a full-scale assault on Messina. Tancred got the message, returned Joanna's dowry and bought Richard off. Philip Augustus was understandably alarmed by his partner's violence, particularly since it had been aimed at a nominal ally. Both armies wintered in Sicily and set sail for the Holy Land in spring 1191.

Philip Augustus enjoyed a calm passage, but Richard was not so lucky. His fleet was blown off course towards Cyprus, where the political situation was tricky. The place was nominally part of the Byzantine Empire but was held by a pretender, Isaac Comnenus. Presumably he thought these were imperial vessels come to eject him, and he reacted accordingly, capturing the family and treating both Joanna and Richard's intended bride, Princess Berengaria, discourteously. Richard was offended and retaliated, imprisoning Isaac and looting his land, untrammelled by any doubts despite knowing that this was both a Christian country and the province of an ally.

Richard reached *Outremer* in June, to find the French and other crusaders besieging the great fortress and port of Acre.

After the rout of Hattin, the surviving crusaders had held on by the skin of their teeth in Tyre, led by the talented Conrad of Montferrat. The useless Guy had been released in 1188 on parole, which he then promptly broke; the church was happy to confirm that a pledge given to a Muslim wasn't binding. Saladin had probably foreseen this and calculated Guy was such a liability he'd do more damage at large. Indeed, Guy had tried to assert whatever remained of his authority over Conrad, who was not in the least impressed. A feud brewed up in the reduced ranks of the crusaders, now split into two factions.

Though Guy had planned to lay siege to Tyre, even he saw how unwise it would be to destroy whatever was left of Christian chances, so instead he gathered his knights and set off to attack Acre. His attempt at an assault failed, but Saladin couldn't dislodge him completely. The crusaders were ringing the city but were themselves besieged by Muslims. Conrad had, at least temporarily, buried the hatchet and reinforced Guy. Philip Augustus had joined both and now Richard arrived. The French had built some enormous siege engines and generally tightened the noose on the city, but there was a marked shortage of action. Richard assumed command, though run down with fever. Thereafter, day by day, the missiles flew and gaps appeared in the city walls. Saladin was just as energetic, sending out skirmishers and launching a series of diversionary attacks to take pressure off the defenders.

Stalemate

As the hot, dry summer burned, neither side was winning. Repeated assaults were thrown back; Richard was still too ill to lead in person. The walls were held by 6,000 defenders but with the English fleet sealing off the seaward side, they were effectively blockaded. At the start of July, Saladin, realizing the situation was desperate, launched an all-out attack, aiming at a final break through. Richard saw off the attempt and sent his own troops in to take the walls. Both failed but the defenders were exhausted. The castellans offered generous terms: release of prisoners, return of the true cross and a hefty indemnity. Richard could enter the city on condition the surviving garrison was spared. He agreed.

Saladin was not at all happy but by now the surrender was complete and the battered, emaciated defenders marched out. As soon as the crusaders got inside, they wasted no time in falling out. Richard championed Guy while Philip Augustus backed Conrad. The Duke of Austria, commanding the Teutonic element, thought his standard was good enough to fly alongside those of the two kings. The English disagreed and threw the

German's banner contemptuously into the ditch. Richard would come to regret this particular insult.

To end the rift, Guy was awarded the crown for the duration of his life – after his death, it would revert to Conrad or his heirs. The Austrian Duke, still fuming at his humiliation, finally went off in a sulk, followed on July 31 by Philip Augustus. As far as he was concerned, the capture of Acre was a success, and he was finding close proximity to Richard increasingly irksome. Richard, for his part, wouldn't miss the French though he was wary of what they might do in Europe while he was away. Although general terms with Saladin had been agreed, the details had yet to be defined.

Some crusader lords had already been freed, though many were still being held captive. Richard demanded their release, though he was not willing to free any of his Muslim captives. Saladin demurred, so Richard, in a fit of rage, had all of his captives – at least 2,500 of them, along with their families – ritually slaughtered in sight of the enemy outposts. As war crimes go, this was particularly shocking, but the church thoroughly approved. They were only infidels, after all.

Jerusalem

Richard had come to "free" Jerusalem, and he wasn't leaving until he knew it was safely within Christendom. Philip Augustus had departed but he'd left many of his knights behind to continue the fight. At the end of the sweltering summer, the crusaders marched out along the Mediterranean shore, leaving only their landward side exposed. Richard kept his men well in hand; to struggle or fall out was to die. Saladin's skirmishers clung like locusts, ready to pounce. The hot breeze was less awful than in the interior and the pious waft of sung psalms rippled down the lines. They marched past Haifa and Mount Carmel, struggling on towards Caesarea. It took two weeks to cover three-score miles and that brought them to Arsuf. Richard had been careful, not exposing or exhausting either his knights or their destriers. They were in prime condition and ready to fight, which was just as well.

It was now September 7, 1191 and Saladin was blocking the coast road south. We really don't know the relative strength of either of the armies: it may be Richard commanded a thousand knights with as many archers and dismounted men-at-arms. Saladin led considerably more overall, though in qualitative terms his light horsemen were outclassed by Christian heavy cavalry. Lionheart formed his lines with their backs to the Mediterranean Sea, facing east. His shock troops, Templars and those French knights Philip Augustus had allowed to remain, formed the right, while the Anglo-Normans covered the center and left. A screen of infantry and bows formed the front line, with baggage and reserves massed along the shore behind. The settlement of Arsuf lay just south, a belt of humped dunes to the north.

Hugh of Burgundy commanded the French contingent. King Guy was there too, and the Grand Master led the Knights of God personally. Saladin's troops faced west, ready to drive the crusaders into the sea – a vast panoply of floating silk banners, braying horns – riot of color. Battalions of skirmishers, thick as mosquitoes, were thrown out in front, lapping around the crusaders' left flank. Though the armies were drawn up early, Saladin waited until the relentless sun climbed higher, dust and steam rising as men and horses waited.

At around nine o'clock in the morning, the Muslim infantry suddenly moved forward. The Christian front line shuddered and then steadied, men raising shields to protect their faces. The knights behind were safe in mail. Arrows hummed and thumped, spitting out of the bright blue sky. The assault was delivered in waves, coming close but avoiding contact. Almost without warning, the masses of footmen would suddenly part, like the Dead Sea, and hordes of light cavalry would surge through the gaps. But the king and his men held fast. Like breakers crashing on the shore – a collision of steel and flesh – the crusaders saw off every charge, English bows and bills taking a heavy toll.

The battle of Ascalon in 1099, depicted in a glass painting in Saint-Denis.

This kind of attrition wasn't to the Templars' liking; they wanted to counter-charge and shatter the enemy line. Richard refused to give the order, preferring to allow the Muslim horsemen to tire themselves out, let their morale begin to sag and losses begin to tell. The Grand Master grew impatient but obeyed his orders to stand firm.

The fight had now lasted several hours when a pair of Templar knights broke ranks and surged after the retreating cavalry. More followed. Everyone now assumed the order to advance had been given. Richard realized there was no chance of recall, so spurred forward.

Hundreds of Saladin's men were skewered or ridden down, while others fled. The defeat at Hattin hadn't been wiped away but it had been avenged. The loss was a heavy one and the myth of Saladin's invincibility had been shattered, but the Muslims' strength still wasn't broken.

Having cleared the way, Richard led the victorious crusaders on to Jaffa, which he occupied and re-fortified to create a safe naval base. Saladin assumed he'd make a dash for Jerusalem so had established a blocking position at Ramleh while his own sappers worked on the city's walls. Once he realized Jaffa was gone, he slighted the walls and buildings of Ascalon, destroying the structures to render them unusable by the enemy. Richard's men, exhausted and flush with victory, were in no mood for further tough campaigning. Cyprus was restless and Conrad was becoming increasingly powerful. It was time for talking.

Saladin thought so too, and let his brother al-Adil negotiate on his behalf. The talks dragged on for 12 unproductive months. Richard was not a natural diplomat and was initially unaware that his wily opponent was also having secret and separate meetings with Conrad.

In November, Richard upped the stakes by launching a thrust at Jerusalem, but the weather was against him, and he had to content himself with rebuilding Ascalon. Meanwhile back at Acre, the Genoese (pro-Conrad) and Pisans (pro-Guy), were at each other's throats. Richard had more to worry about when he learned that brother John in England was talking to Philip Augustus. In an effort to deal with the rival crusaders, he decided to dump Guy and back Conrad, placating the snubbed Frenchman with the gift of Cyprus. Conrad, who was also Guy's brother-in-law, looked set to take the throne. However, his luck ran out and he became the first "celebrity" victim of the shadowy cult of the Assassins. His young widow, still only 21, was quickly married off (for a third time) to Henry of Troyes. Both Richard and Philip Augustus were his uncles.

Richard was running out of time. With trouble brewing back home, he couldn't stay in *Outremer* much longer. Towards the end of May 1192, he marched again on Jerusalem, taking Daron, south of Gaza, by a lightning stroke, and on June 7 set off from Ascalon. Just five days later he reached Beit-Nuba. Despite these successes, it soon became clear to Richard that he would not be able to take back Jerusalem. Even if he could take the city, he wouldn't be able to hold onto it.

Legend insists that the king, as he sent out patrols, led one to a hilltop near Emmaus and there for the first and only time he caught a glimpse of the Jerusalem; the sacred heart of Christianity that he had dedicated himself to recovering. It must have been a bitter moment. The greatest knight of his age, who might have been immortal as the man who won back Jerusalem, could only look on in disappointment. Richard was petty, vengeful and exceedingly cruel, but his piety, like that of his contemporaries,

Black Agnes, from H. E. Marshall's 1906 children's book, Scotland's Story.

was real. It must indeed have been an instant of despair and, from that moment, *Outremer* was on borrowed time.

Not quite a century later, on May 18, 1291 the Sultan al-Ashraf Khalil led the final assault on the last crusader fortress of Acre. Those last, lost crusaders fought hard. They abandoned the ravaged outer wall to try to hang onto the citadel and the aptly named Accursed Tower. Templar and Hospitaller fought shoulder to shoulder. The tower was taken. Both knightly orders, normally less than friendly, launched concerted counter-attacks, immensely brave and determined but the enemy were too many. The inner walls couldn't be held, the attackers burst through. The defenders fought street by street, house by house. The survivors fell back to the port where anyone who could got onboard a ship, (whose captains did a roaring trade selling safe passage out). Those still alive were sold off as slaves. The Kingdom of Heaven had fallen.

Profile: Agnes, Countess of Dunbar and March

If you think chivalry is a man's world, you've clearly never heard of Black Agnes (c. 1312–1369). She's called "Black Agnes" because her lustrous hair was very dark. Agnes had a good patriotic pedigree: her father, Thomas Randolph, Earl of Moray, was Bruce's nephew and a highly successful commander and her mother Isabel was a Stewart. She married Patrick, 9th Earl of Dunbar and March, a leading Scottish magnate.

In 1338, while Agnes was in charge as chatelaine, an English force laid siege to the great coastal fortress of Dunbar. Agnes commanded only a handful of defenders, but was determined to fight:

> Of Scotland's King I haud my house, I pay him meat and fee, and I will keep my gude auld house, while my house will keep me.

The Earl of Salisbury, who was commanding the besiegers, ordered his men to lay waste to the fortress with a barrage of missiles from timber-built siege engines. This was probably more of a psychological move than an effective breakthrough attempt, but Agnes effused to be cowed. She ostentatiously stood by the battlements dusting the merlons (the upright sections of the crenellations) after each projectile sheered off. The English responded by building a great siege tower – or "beffroi" – that could overtop the walls and deliver men-at-arms onto the parapet. Agnes's men managed to throw an immense boulder down onto the tower, crushing it before it was completed.

Archers on both sides left fly. The Scots were decent shots and one of Salisbury's close companions was skewered next to him. "Agnes's love shafts go straight to the heart," the Earl joked, but Salisbury soon resorted to bribery, paying off a junior Scottish officer to leave the postern open and unguarded. The canny Scot took the cash but reported straight back to Agnes. When the English commander led his men through the gate, the portcullis slammed down. Salisbury himself jumped back just in time, though others were captured.

Having tried brute force, starvation and skulduggery, Salisbury fell back on terror. He'd captured Agnes's brother John, Earl of Moray, and threatened to string him up if his sister didn't surrender. Agnes casually retorted that while she'd like to spare her sibling, she wasn't about to hand over the keys and if the unlucky John did swing, at least she'd gain an earldom

Statue of Simon de Montfort on the Haymarket Memorial Clock Tower in Leicester.

of her own. In the event, Moray was spared, so Agnes probably knew it was a bluff.

As Dunbar is on the coast, completely encircling the castle and cutting off all means of supply wasn't easy. Salisbury did his best, but Ramsay of Dalhousie managed to cram a company of reinforcements into small boats and ran the blockade. He sneaked his men inside by the sea gate then promptly launched a raid on the English outposts, causing confusion and alarm.

After five long months, Salisbury conceded defeat and lifted the siege.

Came I early, came I late, I found Agnes at the gate…

CHAPTER 3

LONGSHANKS

Such was the murder of Evesham, for battle it was none.
Robert of Gloucester

ON A HUMID SUMMER'S DAY IN 1265, a fierce electrical storm added a Wagnerian flourish to the high drama being enacted just outside the town of Evesham. Henry III of England found himself a helpless spectator to the furious battle being fought for control of his kingdom. The puppet of the rebel baronial faction, he had been led onto the battlefield in full harness and now wandered aimlessly about as the violent finale of the Second Barons' War exploded around him.

I am Henry of Winchester your king, do not kill me!

Unrecognized in the frenzy, he was wounded in the shoulder, but eventually rescued by his eldest son.

Kings and barons

Barely a year before, when the king had raised his standard at Oxford, he was well positioned to deal a significant blow to his rebellious barons. Their leader – his brother-in-law, Simon de Montfort – had his chief strength in the south, where he held both London and the critical fortress of Dover; and in the Midlands, centered on his great base at Kenilworth.

Henry moved first against the barons' centers at Northampton, Leicester and Nottingham. All three fell like dominos. The king should then have focused entirely on London – to win the capital was to win the war. But he hesitated, and de Montfort grabbed the chance to strike at Rochester, a key royalist outpost.

Rochester was well defended, but King Henry, instead of ignoring the siege and striking at London, swept around in a vast flanking maneuver to relieve the town. He seemed to forget about London and began destroying rebel strongholds in the south-east, finishing his march at Lewes. De Montfort, a canny strategist, realized that in order to win he had to destroy the king's field army. On May 14, 1264, the armies clashed at Lewes. Henry had a poor reputation as a general and although Prince Edward cleared de Montfort's London bands from the field, the Royalists were decisively defeated and the barons won the first round. Henry was a virtual prisoner, and the mantle of power now passed to his son, Edward (known as "Longshanks" on account of his height and long horseman's legs). Edward Longshanks was a very different man to his father – dynamic, charismatic and a brilliant tactician.

Royalist resurgence

In the spring of 1265, all seemed calm, and royalist outposts were few and scattered. But the greed of Simon's sons and the oppression of his virtual dictatorship won few friends. Edward was nominally quiescent, bound by his father's surrender, yet on May 28 at Hereford, he slipped the leash. Royalist lords were mustering at Ludlow. De Montfort was wrong-footed; he was torn between hunting down rebels and falling back to a more central position.

Prince Edward displayed decision and energy, characteristics so lacking in his father, and began a fast-moving campaign. He took Gloucester in mid-June while Simon parlayed with the Welsh Prince Llewellyn, petitioning for his support. The Welshman was enthusiastic; any chance to strike at the marcher lords was welcomed. Now de Montfort could focus on relieving

The Great Tower at Kenilworth Castle, Warwickshire.

his allies still holding out in Gloucester's castle. After finding the road at Monmouth Bridge blocked, his only option was to arrange for a fleet of transports to ferry his troops over the Bristol Channel. Yet Edward now controlled all the Severn crossings.

Worse, Longshanks sent his own small flotilla to take on Simon's transports, and they virtually destroyed the whole fleet. The barons were now the hunted, desperately seeking to get back to Hereford and find a way into England. Simon reached the town on July 20, his army footsore, demoralized and hungry. The only good news was that his son, the young Simon and his units, previously deployed far to the east, were marching to his aid. Edward fell back to keep his grip on the Severn crossings. Simon was still penned in, but the advance of his relief from the south east implied the Prince was in danger of being boxed in by two rebel armies.

Where was Simon the Younger? He'd certainly not displayed any of his father's energy on the march east to his fortress of Kenilworth but it would be reasonable to surmise that contact was, at some point, established. Evesham (once Simon had finally got across the Severn) did appear to have been chosen as the hub. This was eminently sensible as the town lay mid-way between their two forces. From there, two major arterial routes led from Worcester, the Royalists' base, towards both London and Oxford. If Edward wanted to break out of the west to march south and east then Evesham was the obvious starting point. By dusk on the last day in July, the baronial forces at Kenilworth with Simon the Younger were well at ease. Altogether, the army was too large to be easily accommodated inside the walls so many were billeted more comfortably in the town. Simon himself, with some of his entourage, took lodgings within the priory.

Secrets and spies

One of the most tantalizing aspects of medieval warfare is that we learn little from the chroniclers about intelligence. Armies employed spies of course, but Prince Edward appears very well-informed – far more so than his opponents.

One of Simon's household knights, Ralph of Arden was in fact one of two Royalist agents. The other, known only as "Margot," was able to slip out of Kenilworth disguised as a page and alert the Royalists at Worcester. Edward gained an invaluable insight into his enemy's dispositions and their plan for a rendezvous at Evesham on August 4.

Longshanks was not one to let such a golden opportunity pass: he decided on a raid against Simon the Younger at Kenilworth. Attacking enemy quarters is a high-risk strategy that requires boldness, dash and a fair measure of luck. Edward, however, now knew two things vital for success. One: his enemies were unprepared, and two: their forces were dispersed throughout the town. He was aware precisely where each of the rebel officers was billeted. Immediately, he mustered his forces, and wary of Montfortian spies in his own ranks, let them think the plan was a northward movement aimed at Bridgnorth, Shrewsbury or Stafford. The roads to all three passed through Kidderminster, but Edward did not turn left at the crossroads as he should have done. He forked right at Barbourne, barely a mile outside Worcester. This road led directly to Kenilworth.

The lie of the land

From Worcester to Kenilworth is about 34 miles (55 km), while Hereford lies 27 miles (43 km) beyond the Royalist base. Simon the Elder probably received confirmation of his son's arrival at Kenilworth sometime on the 1st of August. With confidence restored, he marched out immediately, probably during the short summer night, and finally managed, after so much frustration, to get over the Severn near Kempsey, barely 4 miles (6.5 km) south of the Royalists. Edward however was, that night, marching northwards. This was a commando raid, not an offensive; Edward's prime objective was to capture the barons in their beds and he knew exactly which beds they would be in. By taking rather than killing the rebel lords, he stripped Simon the Younger's army of all its officers at a single stroke. As a fighting force, this wing of the combined baronial armies would be neutralized. Simon the Younger would still have forces to command but Kenilworth was as fatal to the rebels' cause as Evesham. Edward's raid had been a resounding success.

Simon the Elder would be a much tougher nut to crack. There is a measure of confusion as to his movements in those first, crucial days of August. Some authorities claim that the earl left Kempsey on August 3 and marched the dozen and more miles to Evesham that day. The current view, however, based upon new interpretations of the chronicle sources, is that the advance to Evesham only took place through the hours of darkness during the night of August 3 and morning of August 4 and that the baronial army arrived at Evesham on the morning of the 4th, just prior to the battle. By the evening of the 3rd, Simon would have been aware of his son's defeat. He would have viewed this as a setback rather than a disaster. Simon the Younger's army was beaten but not destroyed:

[he had] lost not all his power … but kept a great host.

There was no reason why he could not lead forces to Evesham for a juncture on the 4th. The town itself would, in any event, be a sensible staging point if de Montfort intended simply to march toward Kenilworth and join his son there.

The calm before the storm

For the whole of August 3, or at least during the daylight hours, neither army moved. Some writers find this anomalous. Yet, certainly in the case of the Royalists, the men desperately needed rest. The infantry may not have marched far (their role had been diversionary) but the cavalry had ridden the hard miles to Kenilworth, fought a sharp fight and then ridden back to Worcester. Neither men nor horses would be ready to deploy again so soon. Simon the Younger's forces had been depleted, but not destroyed. If the Earl reached them, the Montfortians would combine into a very substantial army. The Royalists had no grounds for complacency: Robert of Gloucester tells us that the army from Kenilworth (notwithstanding losses) had, by the

Evesham is remarkable in that it is surrounded on three sides by the Avon. The northern approach is the only clear access; it is at the top of the rise that the three roads coming in from Alcester, Worcester and Stratford all join. Though no evidence of rig and furrow has been detected, it's possible the terrain was farmed. The area beyond was likely common pasture; easy ground on which to deploy troops.

morning of August 4, advanced as far as Alcester, just nine miles north of Evesham. Had the younger Simon possessed his father's drive and energy, events might have panned out differently.

Through that short summer night, the heat of the day still heavy on the roads, the baronial army moved. If we assume a marching speed of 2.5 miles per hour (4 km/h) then reaching Evesham at first light would have been no great hardship. Their route would have taken them along what is now the A44, crossing the Avon firstly at Pershore and then again by the bridge at Evesham, standing south-east of the abbey complex. On reaching the town, Earl Simon, together with the captive king, heard mass. On Henry's insistence, they took some modest refreshment. Simon, unbendingly austere, at first demurred. He had other preoccupations.

Effecting union with his son's forces was just part of his intentions. The other was to put some distance between himself and the royalists who, he still blissfully believed, were at Worcester. The 4 miles (6.5 km) between there and Kempsey had been far too close for comfort. Over the past weeks, the morale of his men had been severely tested; bad news from Kenilworth wasn't likely to raise anyone's spirits.

Strategy

Edward had two key objectives and both were urgent. He needed to prevent a junction of his enemies and bring Earl Simon to battle on favorable terms as soon as possible. An advance to Evesham, if properly timed, would thrust the royalists between the two baronial forces, frustrating any juncture. If he moved fast and took the high ground east of the settlement, Simon de Montfort the Elder was doomed.

In the mid-13th century, Evesham and its abbey were nestled against the head of the loop of the Avon. The religious complex with its attendant, parochial chapels was the most distinguished building by far. Parklands stretched down to the river with the streets concentrated just north of the abbatial precincts, around the bridge at Bengeworth. This key crossing was the only way in for an army coming from the south. If the bridge was sealed off, any defenders inside the town would be forced to either fight or attempt to break out northwards. Simon did not intend, in the early hours of August 4, after his men had just marched all night, to fight a battle. He had no *particular* aversion to fighting, but the odds would not be evened until he'd joined up with his son. For the time being, he just had to keep out of reach of the royalists.

Eminent military historian Sir Charles Oman accepts that Edward had divided his army into three corps and that these advanced through the hours of darkness on the night of August 3 to August 4. He suggests that, by first light, they too were approaching Evesham and that the Prince came from the north (Worcester–Flyford–Dunington–Norton). Gilbert de Clare marched on his right, coming in from the north-west, (Worcester–Wyre–Craycombe), while Roger Mortimer came up on the western flank, (Worcester–Pershore–Hampton).

Nicholas Trevet, a near-contemporary chronicler, tells us Prince Edward marched from Worcester crossing a river by a settlement he calls "Clive." This hamlet has since been associated with Cleeve Prior on the Avon. The place is some 15 miles (24 km) east of Worcester and 5 miles (8 km) north-east of Evesham. There was a ford here and the Evesham–Stratford–Kenilworth road ran through. That the army was divided into three marching corps is supported by Walter of Guisborough, Trevet and the Evesham Chronicler; the latter source that these several axes of advance effectively penned the earl's forces within the town and the encircling loop of the Avon.

The road which passes through Cleeve Prior leads to Kenilworth. By cutting this Edward had effectively blocked Earl Simon's route, supposing de Montfort was intending to head for Kenilworth. If his objective was Alcester then this road too would have to be controlled – to cover one and not the other was pointless. It is generally accepted that at or before Cleeve, de Clare's corps was detached to approach Evesham via the Alcester road. Common sense would validate this. Thomas de Wykes provides confirmation when he states that one corps of the royal army was hidden from the eyes of the baronial division in Evesham by rising ground – all concur this must refer to Green Hill.

There is less agreement as to the approach of the third royalist corps under Mortimer and the role the marchers actually played in the subsequent battle. The debate is rather convoluted but is essential to our fuller understanding of the high drama about to unfold. It is possible that the Prince, having crossed at Cleeve and detached Clare's corps to cover the Alcester road, reached Offenham on the east bank of the Avon, 2 miles (3 km) north of the town. Here he detached Mortimer's corps to sweep around to the west and close the back door by securing the bridge at Bengeworth. The prince then used the ford and bridge at Offenham to bring his own troops to the west bank and unite with de Clare. Some writers take this view but others point out that Guisborough, one of our chief sources, is emphatic that, from the defender's perspective, Edward's corps approached from the north, Mortimer's from the west and to the rear.

Sir Charles Oman, however, takes the view that Mortimer's force was detached from the outset and marched via a different route, actually following that taken by Simon. This is, at least in part, favored by more modern historians and has much to recommend it. The inherent logic is that though Edward, with his own and de Clare's corps had cut both the Kenilworth and Alcester roads, the trap was not fully set unless de Montfort's only possible line of escape from the town was also sealed off. Had the earl marched north and found his line of advance checked, he could simply turn about and escape south or westwards over the bridge, across which he'd earlier entered Evesham.

This would not be an easy maneuver but it was possible. Earl Simon was a general who drilled and trained his men. Edward knew his formidable uncle should never be under-estimated. Dr. David Carpenter disagrees with Oman: he rejects the notion Mortimer was detached from the start of the night march. If Edward approached along the Flyford–Dunnington road his army would be some 7 miles (11 km) to the north of de Montfort's movement along the Pershore-Evesham route. If this was indeed so, given that these maneuvers took place entirely in the dark, neither army could have any real idea as to the whereabouts of the other.

Dr. Carpenter believes the royalists followed the line of the present B4084 road in the UK. De Montfort came onto what is now the direction of the A44 just before Pershore. This alternative puts the armies no more than 2 miles distant on a parallel course, separated by the river barrier of the Avon. If this was so, and the logic is compelling, then it would be at the village of Fladbury that Mortimer's corps was detached. The wide Avon could be forded at Cropthorne and Earl Simon's army followed as it entered Evesham.

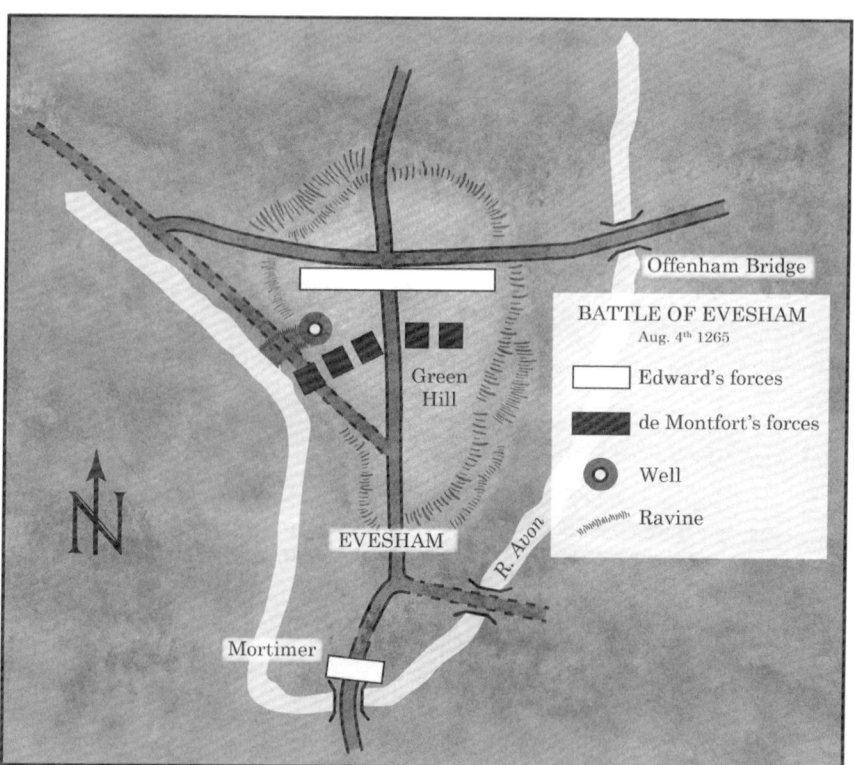

Map 1: The battle of Evesham. (Artwork by Chloe Rodham)

When the royalists left Worcester, there was no clear understanding that Evesham was their goal and to have detached Mortimer at this point would have been tactically unsound. Edward's intention was simple; to shadow and entrap the baronial forces, to match their movement, while giving de Montfort no hint of what they were about. The instant the earl was alerted he'd take steps to slip the snare that was tightening around him. To succeed Edward must delay that moment of awareness until the realization came too late to avert looming catastrophe. He was entirely successful.

Once Mortimer had taken the fork at Fladbury, Edward, with his and de Clare's corps' may have left the line of the B4084 and headed north to cut the Alcester road just short of the hamlet of Norton. De Clare was sent off from here while the Prince's units continued to march for a further 2.5 miles (4 km) to reach Cleeve. Dr Carpenter suggests that the crossings at Offenham was best avoided as this would have considerably increased the risk of observation – even if, by then, it was barely light. Nonetheless, the passage of a large number of armed men would be likely to attract attention in a quiet countryside. Other writers point to the Evesham Chronicler, who insists that the two corps jointly climbed the rise of Green Hill, passing by a venerable stone marker identified as Siflaed's Stone. This was planted 230 yards (210 m) west of the Avon River immediately north of a trackway (now Blayney's Lane) that leads from the crossing at Offenham to the ridge of Green Hill. Clearly this entry suggests that Edward's corps had used the bridge and ford at Offenham.

Royalists vs rebels

In trying to ascertain the numbers on both sides we are forced into the realm of conjecture. Some claim that the royalists enjoyed a comfortable superiority perhaps as high as three to one or even more. That the Prince commanded a significantly larger army is clear. De Montfort was relying upon those reinforcements being brought up by his son and had no intention of giving battle beforehand. His army had endured weeks of hard campaigning and would have suffered reduction through death, wounds, sickness and desertion. True, he had been reinforced by Llywelyn's Welsh spearmen but we have no indication as to their strength. Most writers understandably fight shy of providing estimates. English Heritage, in their *Battlefield Report for Evesham*, suggest that there were 10,000 royalists and 5,000 rebels, with up to 80% ending up as casualties. This does seem rather high and bloody as the fight undoubtedly was, with little or no mercy on offer. It is possible that this figure is on the high side.

This is all conjectural but if we consider that at Lewes the previous year Simon had no more than 500 cavalry (against three times that in the King's army), it is most unlikely he had more at Evesham. We can offer a best guess for overall numbers. Simon may have had 300 cavalry, knights and mounted men-at-arms, no more than 2,500 infantry and perhaps 1,000 Welsh spears. Edward had, say, 4,000 men in his corps of whom 500–700 were mounted. Give Mortimer and de Clare each a total strength of 2,500–3,000 men, perhaps 400–500 of whom were knights. On this basis, the royalists enjoyed an overall superiority of three to one, still two to one if we accept Mortimer's corps played no actual part in the fight itself.

In the glimmer of a summer's dawn the streets were thronged by a horde of footsore, weary men, giving off the collective reek of armies: sweat and unwashed clothing, leather and horse-dung. They'd marched 15 miles, through the hours of darkness over rutted medieval tracks, dried by the sun but layered with thick, clogging dust which would coat the tired men like a leaden shroud. Removed from the hubbub, king and earl heard mass in the abbey, an extensive, well-endowed Benedictine house.

Earl Simon can scarcely have finished his breakfast when scouts came in to report troop movements to the north. Nicholas, the earl's keen-eyed barber, familiar with heraldry, reported seeing the banners of the younger Simon and other Montfortians. He was being fooled: the pennons flaunted were those taken earlier at Kenilworth. Unalarmed, Simon gave orders for his division to form up and prepare to advance. As a safeguard, he detailed the hawk-eyed hairdresser to ascend the abbey tower, looking for any sign of the marchers whom the earl must have suspected were dogging his steps. As he looked this time, Nicholas saw the dummy flags drop and royalist colors raised high.

Worse, Mortimer's corps was also sighted; the back-door was sealed off so only one option other than surrender remained. De Montfort did not falter. He knew himself to be out-classed, out-numbered and without any prospect of safe retreat. It was fight or die. It was still quite early in the morning, but even as the Montfortians hurried to arm themselves, the air, which had been heavy and close, suddenly thickened with darkening skies and an ominous rumble of thunder. Lightning suddenly flickered over the town. Medieval soldiers, deeply superstitious, would have flinched.

Simon led his army out of the town, presumably along the line of the present trunk road. The steady climb continued toward the line of the ridge where the royalists waited. The Earl had deployed his forces with the cavalry leading at the front, the infantry – under Humphrey de Bohun – tramping behind. Many foot soldiers (as well as Llewellyn's spearmen) were Welsh, and none too enthusiastic. Guy Baliol had the honor of carrying Simon's banner. Old King Henry, fully harnessed, rode with the earl, as the other lords followed.

As at Lewes, the Montfortians wore their habitual white crosses on right upper arm, front and back. In lashing rain the dense column of knights made its way up Green Hill, towards the higher ground. It was now Simon recognized de Clare's banner amongst those of his enemies – "that red dog will devour us today," he muttered. He wasn't wrong. Yet, if Simon's position wasn't good, it wasn't yet completely hopeless. If he could punch through the royalist lines then at least a portion of his force might get through to link up with the younger Simon. Evesham might be a Dunkirk rather than a Stalingrad.

Green Hill rises no more than 200 feet (61 m) and we can be sure the main fighting occurred along the ridge-line, though, inevitably, there is some dispute still as to exactly where. The main fight took place where the roads meet, where the east–west axis of High Street meets the north–south line of the Fladbury track (Blayney's Lane). Local tradition records a large number of human bones being found in the land adjoining the old Offenham Bridge, ominously known as "Deadman's Ait."

As the rebels advanced the royalists deployed – this battle would be the classic duel of line versus column. Prince Edward's army formed two wings or battles, astride and flanking the Alcester road, directly barring the rebel maneuver; Longshanks on the left, de Clare on the right. Again, we can be reasonably sure that de Montfort was still advancing with cavalry in front and infantry behind. We are a good deal less certain about the royalist exact deployment. Very possibly it was similar with the mounted arm leading, footsloggers following.

As the heavens opened, de Montfort's cavalry dug spurs for the charge and his squadrons surged forward over the gently rising ground. Lightning forked as the rebel knights came on, the tattoo of the storm rising around drumming hooves. This was the testing point: men and beasts were poised, lances couched and aimed, bracing for the resounding shock of impact. Not so the rebel infantry. Once the Welsh levies saw how strong the opposition looked, their column disintegrated.

Simon's desperate charge had gathered momentum; his mailed horseman struck deep into the royalist line, attacking at the vulnerable junction between two divisions. At this critical point, the earl had greater numbers. If he could break through here, the best part of his cavalry could get clear. Most chroniclers agree that the baronial army drove through those royalists directly in front, sheer élan and mass creating irresistible momentum. The prince's men were forced back in some confusion. It was close, but Simon failed to create a breakthrough. What he did cause was a salient; his charge had driven a wedge into the royalist line.

This was the worst of outcomes. The wings of the prince's army swung inwards like revolving doors. There was no escape for the rebels, who were slaughtered. Henry de Montfort, taking station

Sir John Hawkwood.

beside his father's banner, is said to have led the charge, but was overpowered and killed. More soon piled up around him. With their horses gone, knights fought on foot. Earl Simon was, for a while, shielded by his household men. Despite his age and the hopelessness of their position, the commander-in-chief of the baronial forces made no attempt to escape. As his supporters were systematically hacked down on the blood-soaked ground, the Earl wielded his sword with skill and determination.

His horse was killed beneath him but still he fought on holding his patch of shrinking ground. At least a dozen opponents surrounded the old man, but he would not surrender his sword. It is said one of the common soldiers stabbed the Earl from behind, sliding a dagger between the rings of his chainmail. As he stumbled the merciless blades cut him down. Simon's last words were "*Dieu merci*" (God have mercy). His enemies, in the demonic exhilaration of victory stripped the dead man of armor, clothing and dignity. He was, it is said, still wearing a hair shirt, badge of his undoubted piety. Others went further, including William Maltravers, who savagely mutilated the corpse, cutting off the head, extremities and genitalia. No requiems for Simon.

►——► Profile: Sir John Hawkwood ◄——◄

Sir Arthur Conan Doyle was just the first of a series of writers to immortalize Hawkwood (*c.* 1323–1394) in *The White Company*, published in 1891. There's some doubt as to Sir John's knightly ancestry: he may have been a commoner, or his father may have been a substantial landowner. He seems to have been apprenticed in his youth and may have joined the men of the Grey Goose Feather (as Conan Doyle's poem named those English bowmen) fighting at both Crecy in 1346 and Poitiers, a decade later. Much of his early life is shrouded in mystique and there's a claim it was none other than the Black Prince who knighted him. He seems to have become a mercenary in around 1360, when the Treaty of Bretigny ended that phase of the French wars, joining an infamous bunch called The White Company. Within three years, they'd moved across the Alps and Hawkwood was in charge.

His timing was good. Italy and its city states were riven by infighting following the Papal Schism and Hawkwood's freelance troops were soon spearheading Pisa's war against Florence. By now nearly 40, Sir John did well at the Battle of Cascina, even though he lost. He did rather better at Rubiera in 1372 fighting for Visconti, a Milanese ruler, against the Papacy. His eye for ground and grasp of tactics paid dividends, even if the conflict ended in a compromise. Next, he conducted his great raid on Tuscany. Allegedly in pursuit of cash owed by the Holy See, the mercenaries extracted protection money from every town they came to. Hawkwood made a fortune and sparked yet another bout of strife – the War of Eight Saints.

This one kicked off in 1375 with the White Company under contract to the Pope. While he was a highly effective commander, Hawkwood essentially served only himself. He was heavily implicated in an atrocity, the Massacre of Cesena, but left papal service to join the Milanese and Florentines. Visconti became his father-in-law though they inevitably quarrelled and his last decades were spent in the service of the slippery Medici and wealthy Florence. Hawkwood did very well indeed out of all these wars, buying up estates in both Italy and England. Even in his sixties he was still leading armies and won what is regarded as his finest victory at Castagnaro during the war between Padua and Verona of 1385–1386. He last wore harness fighting against Milan from 1390–1392.

Robert the Bruce being crowned (modern tableau based on facial reconstruction).

At the end of his life he was apparently contemplating retirement to England. This was probably wise, as the catalogue of his enemies in Italy would have filled a whole *Who's Who*. When he died on March 17, 1394, his adopted city of Florence awarded him a state funeral. So great was his fame by this point that Richard II requested his body be returned from Italy to his native shore.

The reality was that Hawkwood was about as far from Chaucer's definition of a "gentle knight" as could be. He was calculating, ruthless, vicious and motivated by opportunism. Legend has it that, while riding through Florence one day, he is said to have responded to a friar's entreaty for charity by tossing him a few coins. The priest thanked him and prayed God might bring him peace, whereupon Hawkwood seized the cash back. Peace, he snorted, was of no interest – he only made money out of war.

CHAPTER 4

BRAVEHEART

Here after ensues the true encounter or
Battle lately done between England and
Scotland: In which battle the Scottish
King was slain.
The True Encounter

IT ALL BEGAN TO GO WRONG as far back as 1286 when Alexander III, middle-aged king of Scotland, ignored advice about the dangerous storm raging around the gables of his council chamber in his haste to meet his dynastic obligations with a teenage bride. His reckless haste proved fatal; unseen he tumbled to his death by the shore and left his kingdom without a king. As the specter of civil war stalked the land the Scots Parliament turned to Longshanks to adjudicate on the rival claimants. On the face of it, this seemed a sensible choice: Edward was the dead king's brother-in-law as well as a leading European statesman and jurist. His assistance, however, came at a price.

Quite simply, whoever was chosen must kneel and pay homage to Edward, acknowledging the English as overlords. This was nothing new: the Saxon kings had attempted sway over Scotland, and William I had extracted something similar from Malcolm Canmore in 1072.

Longshanks settled on John Balliol as Alexander III's successor, and initially the new king of Scots proved malleable. Yet driven by his increasingly dissatisfied nobles, King John was eventually forced, almost certainly unwilling, into acts of defiance against the English, such as concluding a treaty with the French.

Retribution was swift and decisive. Berwick-upon-Tweed, Scotland's most active port, was stormed and razed to the ground, with many inhabitants put to the sword. This savagery set the tone for the next 300 years of virtually continuous enmity. Edward planned to turn Scotland into a province, much as he'd done in Wales, emasculating the indigenous magnates and stamping his authority through an army of occupation. If he thought the job done, then he was deluded. First William Wallace (c. 1270–1305) and then Robert the Bruce (July 11, 1274–June 7, 1329) fought ferociously for Scottish freedom, and while their attempts may, at times, have come up short, they and their countrymen would not surrender to the English.

After the defeat of Longshanks's hedonistic son and successor – Edward II – in 1314, it was the turn of northern England – particularly Northumberland and Cumberland, the two most northerly counties – to feel the weight of Scotland's resurgent power. Bruce's lightly armed raiders, experienced guerrillas who could outwit the more cumbersome English forces launched a series of devastating attacks, levying what we now call blackmail. Such payments bought communities a moment of respite but turned the war into a profitable enterprise, a cottage industry for the Scots. These fast-moving, light cavalry were called "hobilars" and their descendants would be the notorious "Steel Bonnets." They looked like warriors for the working day yet their officers were usually gentlemen. It was said at Pinkie in 1547 that English knights couldn't tell the difference between Scots gentry and commoners, so similar was their kit.

During the course of the following reign, that of Edward III, the wasted upland dales of Northumberland were re-settled by hardy adventurers who held their lands on purely military rather than farming tenure. These settlers came to fight, not farm. For them, war – be it full scale conflict between nations, or what we would now term "low intensity conflict" – became the norm. Learning from the Scots example, the dalesmen moved fast and light, mounted on sturdy ponies, able to live off the land. No great lumbering columns of supply, no flowing silk pennons, no blazons of chivalry – just business. Getting them to fight provided no difficulties; persuading them to turn swords into ploughshares proved considerably more problematic.

The Disinherited

When Robert the Bruce eventually made peace with the English in 1328, he did not take into account the feeling of those English knights who lost their Scottish lands as a consequence of the resulting treaty. A determined faction known as the "Disinherited" arose as an opposing political force. Also less than satisfied was young King Edward, who was unhappy with the peace which had been brokered by his mother and her lover, Roger Mortimer. The young king had since taken the precaution of beheading Mortimer; he quietly supported the Disinherited.

The Disinherited invaded Scotland with a tiny force in 1332. The Scots thought they were a joke, but quickly stopped laughing once the English destroyed their army, the fearsome longbow coming into its own. The dead on the battlefield at Dupplin Moor were said to have been piled as high as a spear's length – over six feet. Edward Balliol, son of the unlamented John, was now crowned king. The young David II, son of Robert Bruce, was spirited to France for safety.

Ed and Dave

Young Balliol's hold on the throne was shaky; even at the coronation feast, the guests remained in full harness, just in case they had to fight for their supper. Not long afterwards, Balliol was swiftly chased out of the kingdom, fleeing in only his nightshirt and one shoe. Edward III now intervened to support his protégé. He laid siege to Berwick and gave the Scots another good hammering at Halidon Hill – an event the old soldiers reckoned evened the score for his father's miserable defeat at Bannockburn.

Life for the Scots became difficult once more: the English army swarmed across the land and Balliol enjoyed a second, equally brief, tenure as puppet king. Within a few years, Edward was bored with Scotland. He was looking across the Channel at a far greater prize, the throne of France, to which, through his mother, he had a claim. Balliol was soon ousted again and in 1341, David II returned to occupy the throne of Scotland. His loyalty to his adopted country, France, proved to be very strong and, five years later, he responded to appeals from the king of France to open a "second front" against the English, who had just trounced the French at Crecy.

This turned out to be a mistake. David's invasion started well (insofar as such things can go "well"), but he ran into trouble just outside Durham at Neville's Cross. The northern English came out to fight the Scots invaders and defeated them. King David, wounded in the face by arrows, took refuge under a bridge as his army began fall apart. An English knight called John Coupland took him prisoner, but not before the struggling king had knocked out a couple of his teeth. He spent the next 11 years in captivity until he was finally ransomed by his subjects in 1357.

Overall, David's reign was not a great success. He had many difficulties with his nobles. His troubles were made worse by the murder of his beautiful mistress, Katherine Mortimer. She was stabbed to death as she rode on the highway, tumbling lifeless from the saddle. This was believed to have been at the order of the king's uncle, Robert the Steward, who was jealous of Katherine's influence over his nephew. When David died, suddenly and without having produced an heir, it was the ageing uncle who took the throne as Robert II: the first of the Stewart

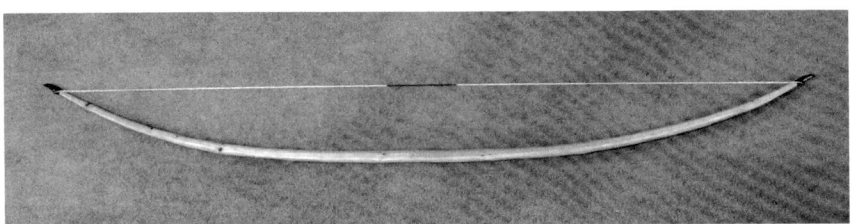

English Yew longbow: 105 lbf, 32 inches.

kings of Scotland who were to reign until the final expulsion of James II of England (VII of Scotland) in 1688.

The first Stewarts

The war with England resumed. The Scots wanted the safe return of their land and castles in the Borders, which the English had occupied since Edward Balliol's day. There was a younger and more confident generation of Scots commanders – including the Earls of Douglas and March – who steadily clawed back lost ground. March's victory over Harry Percy at Otterburn indicated how effective this renaissance had become. James I, Robert III's son, spent much of his youth as a "guest" of the English, having been kidnapped at sea on his way to France. Even when he regained his throne as an adult, it was never secure. He fell out with a powerful clique of lords who launched a raid on the King in his castle at Stirling. A feisty lady-in-waiting barred the door to the royal chamber by thrusting her arm through the socket that normally held the wooden bar.

Surprisingly, the **"reivers"** (raiders) were not natives of the Borders. During the 14th century, in an attempt to repopulate an area rendered a dangerous economic desert by Anglo-Scots warfare, Edward III of England and his counterpart in Scotland encouraged what we would term "relocation" to the border region. The people chosen were hard cases, able to look after themselves and quite happy to do so.

Border reivers at Gilnockie Tower, from an original drawing by G. Cattermole.

It took a few minutes for the attackers to work out how to break through the door, during which time the king prised up several floorboards and dropped into the vault below. One of the attackers worked the blade of his sword into the gap in the jamb of the door and, with a downward stroke, cut off the poor woman's arm. Bursting in, they swiftly discovered the king's hiding place and stabbed him frenziedly to death. The queen was injured trying to protect her husband.

The new king, James II, was still a child, and the powerful Douglas family assumed control as regents. James II grew up to hate them. Dominating his youth, they had vast estates, great wealth and rather regal habits. One fateful day, James invited the Earl of Douglas to dinner. This would be risky for the young earl; another nobleman had recently been executed at just such a soirée. Two courses passed without incident but, before the suckets – candied fruit – could be served, the king accused the earl of treachery. This was true of course; Douglas had been making "secret" deals with England behind James's back. When the earl refused to break contact with the English, King James lashed out, stabbing the earl repeatedly before his attendants laid into the dying Douglas with swords and spears to finish him off. This murderous behavior sparked a civil conflict between the king and the Douglases that ended four years later with a humiliating defeat for the crown.

Hobilers and reivers

By the dawn of the 16th century, the upland riders – latterly known as "hobilers" and then, in the reign of Henry VIII, as the "Border Horse" – knew no occupation other than war. The riding names of North Tynedale and Redesdale – Charltons, Robsons, Milburns, Ridleys, Reeds, Dodds, Herons and Halls – hounded Teviotdale and the Merse. Their Scottish contemporaries from Liddesdale – the Armstrongs, Elliots, Bells and Crozers, along with the Scotts, Kerrs, and Homes – reciprocated with gusto.

These border knights – or "Steel Bonnets," as they were later known – fought a never-ending internecine conflict at a local level.

Italian two-handed sword, 16th century.

It was one element in the broader canvas of the long war between the kingdoms, which often took on a European dimension. Scotland had long been an ally of England's old enemy, France. Indeed, in 1512, the "Auld Alliance" between these two countries was extended, and all nationals of Scotland and France also became nationals of each other's countries, a status not repealed in France until 1903. The following year (1513) saw James IV of Scotland attack the English in support of his French allies, who were locked in battle with Henry VIII (1509–1547). The result was the bloody Battle of Flodden, in which the Scottish king, many of his nobles and 10,000 other men were killed. Things did not soon improve.

In exchange for land and low rents, the monarch required military service on demand. The reivers served as *prickers*, light horsemen with considerable skill at reconnoitring and armed engagement. Their region soon became heavily populated, a situation exacerbated by the *gavelkind* inheritance system, which on his death divided a man's land between his sons; the parcels of land thus handed down were too small to provide an honest living. What had seemed a smart move proved disastrous. Like Frankenstein's creature, armed service for tenure developed a life of its own. The unique provenance and nature of the reivers probably accounts for the need for defensive buildings along this border; the fortified *bastles* (farmhouses). No such building for domestic protection appears anywhere else in Britain.

Most reivers would have a **lance**, used for thrusting and throwing at the enemy – and for fishing, too. There is a record of reivers spearing salmon from horseback in the Solway Firth, testimony to their extraordinary skill with this difficult weapon. Perhaps even more ferocious was the **"Jeddart staff,"** originating in Jedburgh. This was a slim, four-foot (1.25 m) blade set into a wooden staff, the blade having both cutting edge and fearsome spike. Another favorite infantry tool was the **bill**, which had a spike, a hook and a single heavy cutting edge. Both at war and on a raid, the reivers would use also a **backsword**, **dagger** and possibly (in the later 16th century) **a pair of hand guns**, although the wheel-lock pistols (or *daggs*) of the time were inaccurate at any kind of distance.

The Northern Marches

The Northern Marches are a remote part of England, far away from the center of power, difficult and expensive to police. Complex mechanisms aimed at keeping order was established as early as 1249, when the Scottish and English governments agreed that the border should be divided into initially four and then six "Marches" – three on each side: East, Middle and West. From 1297, these Marches were controlled judicially and militarily by Wardens.

These Wardens were usually appointed from the south of the country, in order to avoid the obvious possibility of bias for or against the feuding *names* over which they were intended to hold sway. It was the Wardens' duty to see peace was maintained, to administer justice and to deal with "bills" or complaints. Backed up by a staff of deputies, captains and troopers, they tried with varying degrees of success to administer the law, in so doing creating new personal enmities, only increasing murder and further bitterness between the aggressive reivers. In short, they often caused more problems than they solved and most certainly did not implement peace and safety for the borderers. One such Warden was Sir John Forster, a native Northumbrian rather than a Southerner. Sir John was certainly brave. In battle, he was nigh on unbeatable and saved Queen Elizabeth's throne during the rebellion of the northern earls in 1569. He was also totally corrupt and had a finger in every dishonest pie. Still, he lived to be over 100 and was still dodging assassins almost to the end.

After a raid, having taken cattle and lives if there had been resistance, the reivers would set off for the safety of home without delay. Above all else, success lay in the speed with which the sortie and getaway were accomplished. They would be hampered by their spoils: cattle are notoriously difficult to move at speed and it was essential to be familiar with every inch of the landscape so that temporary hiding places and strategic places for ambush were known.

Victims of the reivers had three choices: to make a complaint to the March Warden, to bide their time and look to return the compliment (with interest, if possible), or to mount a *hot trod*. If some time elapsed before the pursuers set out it was known as a *cold trod*. (A "trod" was the name given to the immediate track and pursuit of raiding parties.) Either way, the legality of the trod depended on its taking place within six days of the raid. As George Macdonald Fraser pointed out, "a careful line was drawn, under Border law, between a trod and reprisal raid." If the trod was cross-Border, it was essential to make it clear that a legal pursuit was going on. A lighted turf was to be clearly visible on the pursuers' lance points indicating "open and peaceful intentions." The posse had a legal right to demand assistance from villagers across the Border – trying to prevent the trod was a punishable offense. That was the theory anyway.

The hot trod could easily run into bother. However strict the rules, it frequently ended in a fierce skirmish during which fighters on either side might be killed. The law was not likely to call a trod-follower to account if his rage got the better of him and he dispatched a reiver out of hand. Vigilante justice was frequently the norm; all that might deter a borderer from killing was the possibility – almost certainty – of a sparking a feud.

Kit and clothing

The border knight looked nothing like the romanticized image. He needed special clothing and equipment to go about his dangerous business. First, and most importantly, he needed a horse. Border knights could be called up to fight for their king; their horses needed to be suitable both for light cavalry work in time of war, and for raiding in time of "peace." These *hobblers*, or *garrons* were sturdy and fast, and like Cumbria's hardy Herdwick sheep, they were also cheap to keep. There is evidence that they were not groomed and that they didn't even need to be shod. A garron was capable of

> transporting a man from Tynedale to Teviotdale and back in 24 hours.

To protect their arms and upper legs, reivers' clothing would bear pewter or brass chains, wrapped around four or five times. Lower legs were protected by long, leather riding boots not unlike modern "biker" boots. Dressed in this way, they were able to move quite easily but were likely to be unharmed by slashing swords or thrusting lances. On his head, the reiver would wear a form of helmet called a *burgonet*, in use from the middle of the 16th century. The *burgonet* or *steill bonnett* was a rather more stylish helmet than the earlier *salade hat*, which, in its lightest form, was open and peaked. They offered good protection, having cheek plates and a flared rim at the neck as well as a peak at the front. In time (from about 1580) these were in turn largely superseded by the *morion* or *pikeman's pot*.

Border knights carried a variety of weapons. As Fraser points out, the 16th century was the

> bridge between the medieval knights and men-at-arms, with their heavy armour and weapons, and the age of firepower.

Feud

An already dire situation was exacerbated by the pernicious code of the vendetta, a relentless legacy of murder known as the "feid" (feud). The inhabitants of Liddesdale – the Armstrongs, Elliotts, Bells and Crozers – had a seriously bad reputation, and this town was regarded as the very worst place on the marches. That was some achievement given the competition. The number of feuds the fractious Armstrongs pursued at any one time easily ran into double figures.

Johnnie Armstrong of Gilnockie was one of the more notorious reivers. These days he would have been called a sociopath but in the early 16th century he was only a little bit worse than the rest. The Armstrongs' inhospitable lands were surrounded by open fells, peat bogs and forest. If they were attacked by superior forces, a fairly frequent occurrence, the people would withdraw to the wasteland of the Tarras Moss, a particularly nasty bog where detailed local knowledge was fairly essential unless you wanted to disappear into a mess of sucking mud.

If you did have to abandon your tower there was a handy trick to prevent the enemy from pulling it down ("slighting" as this was called). You stuffed the ground floor with peat and then set it alight. As the floor was a stone vault the place wouldn't burn down but the smoldering peat provided a dense smokescreen that would persist for days. The acrid smoke made it very difficult for an enemy to get near the place.

Life in Liddesdale wasn't easy, nor was it pleasant. Frequently the Armstrongs would ride out on raiding expeditions with their neighbors, depending on whether they were feuding with them at the time. Johnnie Armstrong was a legend in his own, quite short, lifetime. Murder, theft, looting, arson and blackmail were a way of life – indeed, the borderers raised this "lifestyle" almost to an art form. As his crimes multiplied, Johnnie's stature increased, and eventually his name was mentioned at court. The King of Scotland at this time was James V, father of Mary Queen of Scots.

King James determined to bring order to the borders, an attempt to halt a slide into total anarchy. The name of Johnnie Armstrong cropped up with monotonous regularity so he was summoned to appear before James on a truce day. Now the essence of the day of truce was that everyone was safe, nobody could kill anybody whilst the truce day lasted. Johnnie, thinking himself safe, duly appeared, not to ask for pardon but to show off his status as Liddesdale's most successful bandit. He and his chums were dressed in their finest velvet and silks (which had probably begun life as someone else's), their horses beautifully groomed and caparisoned.

This was not a man coming to account for his crimes or to seek royal forgiveness; this was a man who considered himself a master in his own domain, above the law. That fine show was a very, very bad idea. King James, ever quick tempered, was outraged.

The Combat of the Thirty (between Ploërmel and Josselin) in 1351. Miniature from the Compillation des cronicques et ystoires des Bretons *(1480), by Pierre Le Baud.*

He demanded the whole gang be taken into immediate custody. Johnnie tried to brazen it out but his bluster merely added fuel to the fire. Hanging a fellow on a truce day was very bad form indeed but James was sufficiently angry to forget precedent. Soon Armstrong and his accomplices were all swinging gently in the breeze. "Their necks felt the weight of their boots," a laconic observer recorded. Johnnie's judicial murder made a martyr of him. The fine tower attributed to him still stands at Gilnockie, recently restored and beautifully located; a quintessential Scottish gentlemen's border residence, fine ashlar and crisp, crow stepped gables.

These knights from the border marches may not have conformed to any romantic image; there was nothing nice about them or their times but they knew how to fight. Their names, Harry "Hotspur," Black Douglas, Bull Dacre, Sir John Forster and the Bold Buccleuch, have survived and resonate, even if the reality has been up-graded.

←←→ Profile: Gwenllian ferch Gruffydd →→→

The border between Scotland and England was not the only one in dispute: the disputed marches between England and Wales had been a "hot" frontier since before the conquest. Harold had campaigned successfully against the Welsh princes in the 1050s and the Conqueror settled strong warlords along the line. Their remit was simple, take whatever you can hold. They did and there was sporadic warfare along the marches until Longshanks finally tamed the Dragon for good in the 1280s. Gwenllian (*c.* 1100–1136) was the daughter of Gruffudd ap Cynan, ruler of Gwynedd. He married her off to Gruffydd ap Rhys, Prince of Deheubarth. She was the youngest of eight children and a great-great-great-grand-daughter of the great Brian Boru, High King of Ireland, who'd fought his last great battle against the Norsemen at Clontarf in 1014, breaking their power forever.

Gwenllian was, of course, said to be very lovely and the match between her and Gruffydd appears to have been a real romance. They were probably married when she was very young. Her consort was having bother with encroaching Normans filtering into the valleys of South Wales. The pressure was mounting and the young lovers with their diehard followers led an often difficult existence, maintaining a guerrilla-style campaign against

The Hundred Years War, fought between the English royals, the House of Plantagenet, and their French counterparts, the House of Valois, actually lasted for 116 years. The two monarchies disagreed over the line of succession to the French throne, which was an issue of utmost importance, as France was the most powerful nation in Western Europe at the time.

the intruders, striking from forest and mountain bases. What they took from the rich, they were said to give to the poor, like a Welsh Robin Hood and Maid Marion.

Their chance to strike back came with the Anarchy in 1136. Their Norman tormentors were at each other's throats. In the south Hywel ap Maredudd was the first to attack, trouncing the incomers at the Battle of Llwchwr. Gruffydd was encouraged and planned a campaign with Gwenllian's father Gruffudd. His absence in Gwynedd left the door open for a Norman counter-strike, led by Maurice of London, Lord of Kidwelly. She rose to the challenge and raised a force to take him on.

An inspiring leader, she led her men on the great Marcher castle at Kidwelly; the armies met just north of it. Gwenllian was killed, along with one or perhaps two of her young sons during or just after the fight. The area north of Kidwelly was known thereafter as Maes Gwenllian ("the field of Gwenllian"), and a spring is said to have miraculously welled up on the spot where she died. An earthwork on the possible site of the clash is said to be her tomb. Her memory proved a talisman for the Welsh who fought on, defeating and killing Richard de Clare. Her brothers picked up the torch and drove the invaders back from numerous strongholds. "Revenge for Gwenllian" became a great rallying cry; like Boudicca (with whom she's often compared), Gwenllian is now viewed as a tragic heroine.

CHAPTER 5

ST. CRISPIN'S DAY

And let us right there try ourselves and do so much that people will speak of it in future times in halls, in palaces, in public places and elsewhere throughout the world.
Froissart

ON MARCH 26, 1361, IN BRITTANY, between the rival garrisons of Josselin and Ploermel, 30 English and German knights took on 30 Frenchmen. The Hundred Years War was well underway but this was a quixotic mini-battle straight out of Henty or Dumas. The mêlée is a footnote in the seemingly endless civil war in Brittany with the English, under Sir Robert Bemborough, fighting Jean de Beaumanoir's Breton French, each standing for rival factions. There was no real tactical benefit to the clash for either side, but tensions were high and the knights were in the mood to fight. It may be the English had acted the role of heavy handed oppressors and the Bretons came on as deliverers. Bemborough was a protégé of the formidable Sir Thomas Dagworth, who'd been killed in an ambush over a decade before.

A formal duelling ground, the "Half-way Oak," was selected between the two fortresses and set up as for a tournament, with seating for spectators and refreshments on sale. Bemborough had two proven knights, Sir Robert Knollys and Hugh Calveley, on his team though a full third were made up from a mix of Germans and renegade Bretons. The combat was very lively indeed. If the crowd were hoping for blood, they certainly got their money's

The battle of Crécy, from Jean Froissart's Chronicles.

worth. After the first bout, four French and two English knights were down. After tea, in the second half, Bemborough was killed. Despite losing their chief, the English fought on doggedly until Guillaume de Montauban broke their line and went on to get the better of seven opponents. The survivors threw in the towel. Both sides lost heavily in dead and wounded.

The Hundred Years War

If his portrait is anything to go by, Henry V didn't look like a great knightly hero. Yet he, more than any other English king, embodied the ideals of chivalry. He was utterly ruthless and wholly convinced of his own righteousness – that blend of religiosity and casual, utterly cynical brutality that we now find

Street sign in modern Crécy.

hard to grasp. He is said to have quipped that war without fire is like sausages without mustard.

He was valiant, purposeful and generally courteous to those who he thought merited courtesy. He also murdered his prisoners and left refugees from his sieges to starve in No Man's Land. He won perhaps the most famous of all famous English victories at Agincourt. Yet the battle was forced on him in the course of an ill judged and pointless *chevauchée*. He had captured Harfleur in that year, losing far more men to dysentery than enemy action, the same disease that he himself would later succumb to.

Henry didn't begin the war – *La Guerre de Cent Ans* had been going for two generations, having been started by Edward III in 1337. He'd inherited a claim to the French throne from his

The Black Death struck Britain in the middle of the 14th century. Estimates vary as to the number killed – it could be anywhere between 40–60% of a population believed to be around six million. The knightly classes suffered less than the very poor, but were to be affected by the social changes the plague brought with it. They effectively signalled the end of feudalism and, in time, the end of the knightly system.

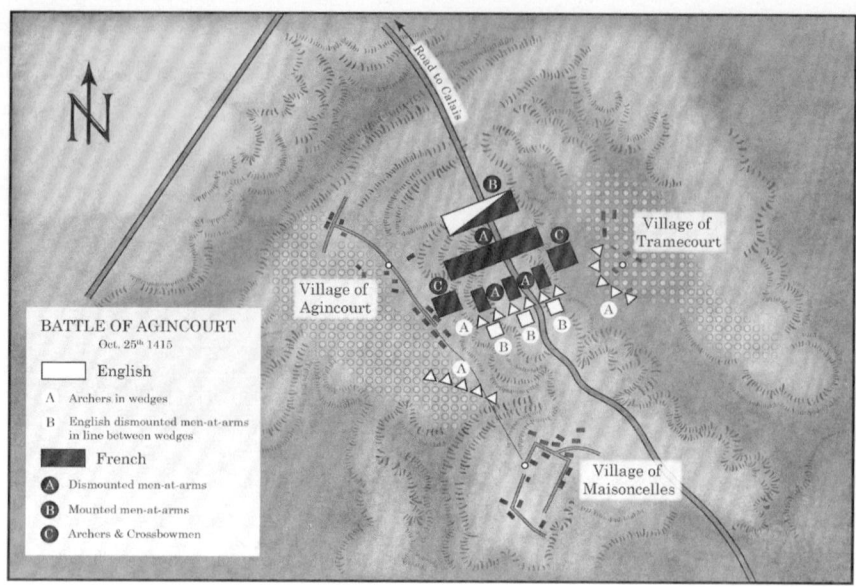

Map 2: The battle of Agincourt. (Artwork by Chloe Rodham)

mother, Isabella of France (nicknamed the "She Wolf"). He'd also inherited her volatile temper. Happily, his military skills were more on a par with those of his grandfather, Longshanks, than his ineffectual father. Edward no longer relied on the feudal host. His was a contract army, waged, professional and tactically innovative. At Halidon Hill in 1333 he'd unleashed the arrow storm against the Scots with devastating results.

France would come to know all about the great English war bow, though it took her decades to overhaul her own tactics. Time and again, the cream of French chivalry would lumber towards the steady lines of bows and bills and be dropped in droves. English knights didn't now fight as individual warriors but as part of a machine, the harrow – or *herce* – formation. Companies were formed up on foot between wedges of archers. The interlocking killing zone created by the spraying effect of massed bows on the flanks and the wedges between was truly terrible.

War with France represented a major military proposition, demanding skill in expeditionary warfare, something that British armies would retain for the best part of seven centuries. It needed lots of money and a round of intense diplomacy to isolate the French king, Philip of Valois. Edward gained grants from parliament, loans from the Hanseatic League, politic subsidies from the church in England, wisely keeping the king on side. He did deals on wool supplies, England's great cash crop. He brokered partnerships and invaded first in 1339 though this first foray achieved little. However, his army was learning, and soon became a tight, professional force that carried all of its own specialists and a vast reserve of munition quality arrows, mass-produced by the crown.

The following year, an English fleet hammered the French at Sluys, giving Edward command of the Channel. He intervened during a civil war in Brittany after 1342, backing a rival to the French king's preferred candidate. A series of small but telling longbow victories followed, and in 1346 Edward landed an English army in Normandy. If nothing else, this relieved pressure on Gascony, which the French were trying to claw back.

When the French army headed north to confront the insolent English, Edward marched towards Flanders. His ships had departed, so no help was available getting his 12,000-strong army across the Seine. He managed it nonetheless, fighting a brilliant action at the ford of Blanchetaque. The inevitable clash of armies came at Crecy on August 26. The French had never savored the full barrage of the arrow storm, and Philip IV was woefully unready. His army attacked as a series of mobs, even riding down their own mercenary crossbowmen. Many were dead long before the survivors came to contact. English knights and billmen finished the job. The killing was prodigious and at least 1,200 French gentry died. This wasn't a chivalric game anymore; English losses were minimal.

Next up was Calais, destined to be England's economic and military bridgehead. It fell to siege in 1347 and would remain in English hands for over two centuries. But nature intervened, interrupting the fighting as both nations reeled from the horrors of the Black Death. Ten years after Crecy, Edward's eldest son, the "Black Prince" of legend, rampaged through central France and, when confronted by a superior force at Poitiers, stood and fought. He won; another spectacular success which netted the hapless King John of France. Chaos descended over France, popular unrest rife as good lordship evaporated and the English pillaged pretty much at will.

Edward gained a lot from the Treaty of Bretigny, sealed on May 8, 1360, but had to abandon his claim to the French throne. King John was released on parole to raise his enormous ransom. This was the high-water mark of this phase of the War: England appeared invincible.

The Black Prince intervened in Spanish politics in 1366, winning yet another big fight at Najera. It was a pointless and hollow triumph however, which gained him nothing. His health was already deteriorating. He died in June 1376 and his father followed just over a year later.

The new king, Richard II, was just a boy and his reign would not be a happy one. He's credited with inventing the pocket handkerchief, but lost most of France. Win some, lose some. A Gallic recovery headed by the resilient Breton knight Bertrand du Guesclin clawed back most of the English gains, almost to the gates of Calais.

Meanwhile, England was facing domestic troubles, firstly from the Peasants Revolt and then from more bother with the Scots. The King's rule went from bad to worse. Though the war in France was going disastrously, the burden of taxation remained high. Richard was finally removed, and almost certainly murdered, by his cousin Bolingbroke, who had himself crowned Henry IV.

Despite their remarkable comeback, the French were equally divided. Charles VI had succumbed to mental illness so the great lords squabbled and jockeyed. The Burgundian John the Fearless bumped off his rival Louis of Orleans. Civil war between his successors, the Armagnacs and the Burgundians, erupted. Both sides were quite ready to bid for English support, their mutual hatred cancelling out any notion of country.

Henry IV enjoyed neither peace nor security. Usurpers rarely sleep easily and he was perpetually strapped for cash. When he died in 1413, few were sad to see him go. His son, Henry V, took the throne. Henry's apparently dissolute youth was immediately put behind him, the low company of his tavern days discarded. This young king was born into battle. The war was about to get hot again.

> But if it be a sin to covet honour,
> I am the most offending soul alive.

At first there was some reluctance: the glory days of Crecy and Poitiers were a long time past. Henry pushed his council for war early in 1414 but they advised caution, *keep talking*. Henry offered to renounce his claim to the French throne if they'd cough up the arrears in King John's ransom and confirm English claims to all disputed territories. Oh, and Henry would marry the French king's daughter, who would bring a hefty dowry with her. Unsurprisingly, the French declined, allegedly sending a sneering gift of tennis balls:

> We are glad the Dauphin is so pleasant with us;
> His present and your pains we thank you for:
> When we have match'd our rackets to these balls,
> We will, in France, by God's grace, play a set
> Shall strike his father's crown into the hazard.

At a council meeting on April 19, 1415, Henry got the thumbs up: parliament had voted to grant a double subsidy. The young king was thorough. He prepared a large fleet to transport some 12,000 fighters and up to 20,000 horses. His first target was the strategic harbor of Harfleur, well located and heavily defended. The siege dragged on through a hot summer as dysentery stalked the English ranks. The place didn't open its gates until September 22, late in the season.

> Once more unto the breach, dear friends, once more;
> Or close the wall up with our English dead.

On the back foot

Given the level of casualties thus far, it might have been best to return to England, but Henry decided instead to march his army through northern France – up to Calais. This raid would serve no strategic purpose – it was little more than a demonstration of aggression. He almost certainly did not intend to fight a major battle. Numbers are uncertain, but the English by this time were between 6,000–9,000 strong.

Meanwhile the French, who'd made no real effort to relieve Harfleur, were mustering at Rouen. As Henry moved north so did they. Led by professional captains who preferred Fabian tactics, avoiding direct confrontation, they soon heavily outnumbered the invaders. They used the Somme as a defensive line and attempted to deny Henry a crossing place. It was now October and time was a luxury the English didn't have. Weakened by disease, increasingly ragged and hungry, Henry's grand gesture began to look more like a trap.

Finally, the English got across at Bethancourt and Voyennes. They were clear of the wet gap if not of their pursuers. It may be the French outnumbered them by as many as six to one – stiff odds, but the English had a habit of surprising the French with their ferocity. The leaders of the French army, professionals like

Perhaps the English bowmen offered the advancing French the traditional **two-fingered salute**. This wasn't just a gesture – there was a rumor that any captured archer would lose those two fingers so he could never draw again. These men had all digits present and in working order.

Boucicault and d'Albret, the dukes of Orleans and Bourbon, were all for caution; illness and famine might do the job for them. Others, hot-blooded young knights who'd never fought the English before, were desperate to win their spurs. On October 24, in a dank and dismal autumn, Henry's tattered band found the road ahead blocked. They would have to fight their way through or accept defeat and surrender.

Agincourt

It's generally, if not completely, agreed (no medieval battle sites ever are) that the fight occurred over a narrow strip of undulating country with the castle and hamlet of Agincourt standing a couple of miles further on. Open ground between there and Tramecourt, hemmed on both flanks by a funnel of woods, would form the killing ground. For what was to be a damp, miserable, hungry and fearful night, the English set up a makeshift camp just west of Maisoncelles. Wet, often ill and with empty bellies, they clustered around sputtering fires. The French camp might be a way off but they could hear the braying of their enemies, full of food and drink, toasting the ransoms they'd win.

Creeping grey autumn dawn rolled in as the English deployed across a front of 750 yards (690 m). As usual, the army was marshalled in three brigades (see map 2). The corpulent Duke of York led the right or vanguard, Henry the middle, with the left under Lord Camoys. Veteran Sir Thomas Erpingham commanded the bows: these were probably massed on the flanks for enfilade effect with dismounted knights and men-at-arms, four ranks deep standing between. Archers planted wooden stakes in front of their lines to break up or at least disorder any mounted charge.

The woods acted like a funnel, so greater numbers would not necessarily be decisive. The French knights thought they would be, so jockeyed for the honor of being in the front, the first of three divisions advancing in line astern. The experienced d'Albret and Boucicault would be in the vanguard, as would many leading gentry. The professionals, such as the constable of France, were dead against such massing of choice targets, but the knights refused to miss out on the fun. There may have been as many as 8,000 men-at-arms and 1,500 crossbowmen in this steel tipped avalanche.

In the second line were more high nobility, the Dukes of Bar and Alencon with the Count of Nevers. Behind them, as a rearguard, another great mass of men-at-arms, led by the Counts of Dammartin and Fauconberg. This third division appears to have been bolstered by a fair few camp followers and servants, hoping for a share of the spoils. It had been a long time since the French had felt an arrow's sting and they had grown contemptuous – had allowed the plight of the English army and their shrunken numbers to blind them. They would pay a heavy price for that disdain. One tactic they had agreed on was to detach two mounted commandos, one on each flank, whose mission was to try and ride down the archers.

In their eagerness, the French knights had not given much thought to the lie of the ground, though they should have. The tunnel effect of forests on both flanks created a narrowing funnel into which they were increasingly jammed. Heavy autumn rain had soaked the fields, now a thick glutinous mud soup. An armored man carried approximately 60 pounds (30 kg) of harness. In addition, most knights wore bascinets with their distinctive "pig-faced" snouts, which limited their vision and impaired their hearing. Each man's view of the battlefield was restricted and he would be advancing slowly on foot through cloying mud.

When drawing up their battle plan, the French marshals had intended first to deploy crossbowmen and whatever archers they had in the first rank to provide a missile shield for the men-at-arms, and second for the two flanking charges to be both powerful and coordinated. This might have worked had the knights not demanded they lead the assault. In the event, it was Henry who decided to commence, as, once his men had drawn up, the French initially declined to attack. Despite their apparent enthusiasm, command and control was minimal. Only when the English moved their whole line forward, almost bringing the French within range did the latter lumber into action. The cavalry wings were unready and uncoordinated. Many of those supposed to mount up and take part couldn't be found or mustered. The mud prevented any semblance of a canter; horses plunged and slid at no more than a walk. By the time they did move, the English had already loosed, slowing the struggling momentum.

Henry had words for his men, recalled and surely embroidered by Shakespeare, a rousing incitement to mass-killing:

We would not die in that man's company
That fears his fellowship to die with us.
This day is called the feast of Crispian:
He that outlives this day, and comes safe home,
Will stand a tip-toe when the day is named,
And rouse him at the name of Crispian.
He that shall live this day, and see old age,
Will yearly on the vigil feast his neighbours,
And say 'To-morrow is Saint Crispian:'
Then will he strip his sleeve and show his scars.
And say 'These wounds I had on Crispin's day.'
Old men forget: yet all shall be forgot,
But he'll remember with advantages
What feats he did that day: then shall our names.
Familiar in his mouth as household words
Harry the king, Bedford and Exeter,
Warwick and Talbot, Salisbury and Gloucester,
Be in their flowing cups freshly remember'd.
This story shall the good man teach his son;
And Crispin Crispian shall ne'er go by,
From this day to the ending of the world,
But we in it shall be remember'd.

Nock, draw, loose – the rapid rattle of command rang out as the French came into range. Each man bent to the draw. The weight required to pull back the string was considerable, needing entire body strength. Despite this immense effort, each man

Memorial to those who died in the battle of Agincourt.

could loose 12–15 arrows a minute. If Henry's archers shot for say ten minutes, that would add up over half a million arrows. Hardened steel tipped bodkins arced towards the French, the panoply of knights contrasting with the workaday yeomen. Many, racked by dysentery, had dropped their hose. What effect this had on the French, we cannot say.

Ploughing forward on both flanks, the French cavalry were already in trouble, as they found themselves prime targets for that blizzard of arrows. A ton of horse going down in the morass, flinging its armored rider or pinning him underneath, wasn't just a casualty, it was an obstacle, slowing those behind. The more they fell, the worse the problem. With trees on their flank, the mounted knights couldn't get around the English bows and the lines of stakes took them by surprise. Some commentators, notably the great Sir John Keegan, take the view that the archers main contribution at this point was in killing French horses.

An arrow isn't kind: the pain of injury is immediate and intense. If a man goes down in the great scrum of knights, he'll be pressed into the viscous mud then trampled or asphyxiated. Somme slime did a lot of the Englishmen's killing for them; centuries later, their descendants would flounder in the same muck. Those high-ranging shots the English dropped at more extreme ranges struck horses, which, maddened by pain, careered wildly across the field. Panicked and rider-less, many crashed into and through the attacking heavy infantry; those that collapsed, iron-shod hooves still thrashing, created significant barriers.

At the outset, perhaps 300 yards (275 m) separated the front lines. We don't know how long it took the French knights to stumble and splodge across the gap. As the range narrowed, they loosed aimed flights on a flattening trajectory. These men were good shots, picking the weak spots – the joints in armor or less protected areas – for maximum effect. Wickedly long bodkins could still punch through a fair thickness of plate, and not all knights would have been wearing top-end steel harness. Many would be wearing armor handed down from their relatives or mentors; this kit was too expensive to discard and therefore remained more vulnerable.

Despite the mauling, the pressure and the mud, the French still came to contact and crashed home with sufficient force to press the English center back. Of course, it may be that the English gave just enough ground to soak up the momentum and imprison the French in a deepening salient, those deadly archers still massed on both flanks. How many French had already died, shot or trampled, is impossible to say, but it was probably a significant number, and by now the survivors were compressed like tinned sardines.

There was no room for the men-at-arms to swing their weapons; most were already disorientated and exhausted. The mêlée became more of a massacre. The English were relatively fresh, well-spaced and ready. The more the French at the rear pushed forward, the more damage they did to those at the front. The men went down in droves, smashed or hacked down into the soup. Asphyxiation, heat exhaustion and drowning probably killed far more Frenchmen than English bills and bows. Longbowmen, having exhausted their ammunition, picked up weapons, even heavy mauls used for hammering stakes, and attacked. This was downright ungentlemanly – French knights had not got dressed up to fight sweaty, unkempt peasant farmers. Knights fought knights for glory and ransom, everybody knew that.

Typically, two archers would target a single man-at-arms: one to block his sword, the other hooking behind the knee, bringing their opponent down. By now the battlefield was a butcher's yard, the French dead sprawling in heaps, so that the living fought on top of mounds of corpses, or near corpses; shuddering, writhing, screaming out, a wailing dismal chorus of agony adding to the great surging noise of battle.

As the front line dissolved, the second crowded on, not realizing they would just add to the mounting piles. The more they came, the swifter they died. How long the actual fighting continued for is uncertain, probably not more than a couple of hours, but in that time thousands died. Hundreds of exhausted and thoroughly demoralized knights were taken prisoner, providing a significant cash bonus for the English, compensation for all their hungry marches.

Henry was in his element. He took his place in the line but used his household men as a mobile bayonet squad to shore up wherever the fighting was thickest. His younger brother, Humphrey, Duke of Gloucester, was wounded and Henry stood over him till the Duke was dragged clear. It was said at least one of the gilded points on the coronet circling his helmet was bashed off. Finally, the English ran out of Frenchmen to kill. The two leading divisions had been dealt with, but the third, ominously, was milling about as though getting ready to weigh in. There would be no respite for the exhausted bows and bills, archers scattered over the field retrieving arrows. It seemed they would be needed.

What might be termed a local tactical success for the French was a successful raid on the English camp. Whether this was indeed a planned tactic or mere opportunism isn't clear. A force, mainly of local levies under Ysembart d'Azincourt, pillaged the English's supplies. He was the local lord with his own tenants and retainers, which is more suggestive of private enterprise than planned strategy. Whether this happened at the start or nearer the end of the fighting is none too clear. The raiders took whatever they could find and made no effort to capitalize on their position. Perhaps it was this, combined with the great bulk of the third French division massing in front, that convinced Henry he was about to be attacked again.

Though there's no proof to support the fact, it was highly likely that it was Henry himself who gave the order to kill the French prisoners. Only he had the authority, and he was certainly ruthless enough. The battle wasn't yet won: the French rearguard alone outnumbered the English and there seemed to be more Frenchmen behind. The killing of the prisoners wouldn't be a popular order, but on economic rather than humanitarian grounds: a dead Frenchman was worth nothing. English knights found this murderous chore beneath them and let the common archers attend to the killing, which, if approached with reluctance, was carried out with gusto. The doomed prisoners were bludgeoned or felled by bill strokes. How many were killed we don't know. At some point, it became obvious the French reserve had no stomach for more fighting and the slaughter was halted.

The "kill-rate" was prodigious. In less than two hours, between 6,000 and 10,000 Frenchmen had died. A great swathe of French gentry, including d'Albret, were killed, alongside three dukes, eight counts and an archbishop. Hundreds of knights perished. The loss fell most heavily amongst the northern gentry, weakening future resistance against Henry's next campaigns. English casualties were nominal, though certainly more than the "five and twenty" Shakespeare counted in his play. The only important English man to die was the Duke of York, probably not killed by the French – he seems to have suffered a stroke.

The battle of Agincourt was a famous victory but it did not win the war; that had the best part of 40 years left to run. Henry took most of Normandy and the hand of Princess Katherine. He very nearly had it all in the bag when, in 1422, at the age of 32, dysentery cut short his glittering career. It was not obvious at the time, but the English king's death marked the apex of the Plantagenet campaign in France. From now on, despite a number of tactical victories, the English were losing the war.

Kings and regents

During the minority of Henry VI (1422–1437) his uncle John, Duke of Bedford maintained the impetus. He and the somewhat Machiavellian Cardinal Beaufort broadly agreed that the correct course was to maintain the steady acquisition of territories and establish the full authority of the English Crown in France. All well and good, but the plain fact was that Henry would be a very poor shadow of his father. Furthermore, bubbling factionalism, like a witch's brew, would hamstring any efforts to extend English influence in France. Any chance the English might have had of winning died with Henry V.

Until the collapse of the Burgundian alliance in 1435 and Bedford's death, final success had still appeared feasible. English armies continued to win more battles, though the arrival of Joan of Arc and the defeat at Orleans showed that success was never a given. The role of the late king's other surviving brother, the mercurial Humphrey, Duke of Gloucester, was restricted to that of protector, defender and chief councillor, a rather shapeless remit. He only obtained authority when Bedford was engaged in affairs overseas, and found himself unable to exercise full control over a council which was increasingly dominated by Cardinal Beaufort.

In 1437, the real difficulties of the reign were not entirely apparent. Despite internal divisions, the council had done much to bolster the English position in France and maintain the rule of law at home. Bedford and Beaufort had seen themselves as legatees of Henry V's policies. They had attempted, not without success, to maintain these, but a holding policy can't be indefinite. At some point a new direction must emerge and this could only come from the person of the king himself. It was time for Henry VI to take control of the affairs of state. And that was a problem.

At this time of mounting difficulties, with the position in France on the point of unravelling, England had a boy king, a divided council and a resentful parliament, whose willingness to continue levying taxes was waning. Cardinal Beaufort, with the Duke of Suffolk and others of his affinity, was in favor of a pragmatic approach; peace with honor. It appeared obvious to the peace faction that England was no longer able to add to her French territories. The pendulum had swung too far the other way. It was more a matter of clinging to whatever gains could be salvaged. Henry VI had, in fact, been crowned king of France in Paris on December 2, 1431, a good show, but something of a sham. The true king of France was always crowned at Reims, where he was anointed with St. Remy's holy oil.

Disappointments

It was rapidly becoming clear to those around the young king that Henry VI had not inherited his father's skills. His finances were already becoming tricky. Fresh campaigns, such as that in Guyenne during 1439, proved difficult to fund. In this new mood of pragmatism, Beaufort attempted further negotiations at Calais in 1439 and offered to release the Duke of Orleans,

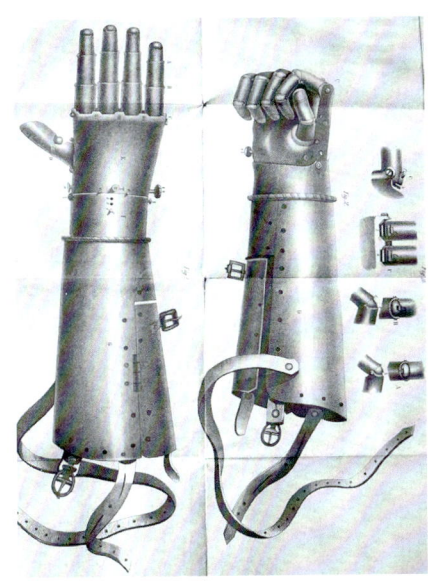

Copper engraving of Götz of the Iron Hand, City Museum of Cologne.

The Iron Hand (Eiserne Hand) of Götz von Berlichingen.

who had languished in captivity since 1415. This was expressly contrary to the late king's policy. Humphrey of Gloucester managed to get the initiative blocked in council. The commons were still loud for the war and Duke Humphrey achieved a measure of popular acclaim, but he and his supporters were blinding themselves.

In the early 1440s, Cardinal Beaufort's influence waned, dented by the failure of the Gravelines conference, which he had hoped would bring important commercial advantages as well as an honorable peace, and Suffolk assumed a more pivotal role. If the Duke was not a great man and prone, like many of his contemporaries, to corruption, he was in a very difficult position. He was trying to carry out policy that should properly have been directed by the king but he was hamstrung by a monarch who appeared disinterested. The Duke of York was sent to France as Lieutenant for a further five-year term in 1440. There is no direct evidence, at this time, that York was in any way out of favor or that he was anything other than a functioning member of the administration. The fatal split would emerge later.

By way of a dynastic marriage, the best that the young king of England could achieve was the hand of the 16-year-old Margaret of Anjou. She was the daughter of Duke Rene of Bar and Lorraine, the titular, if impecunious, King of Sicily, unable even to fund a dowry. This young and spirited princess arrived in England during April 1445. Her sea passage, though her fleet was magnificent, was turbulent and she required several days of rest at Portsmouth. She had yet to meet her new husband, though already officially married a

Edward IV.

month since at Nancy (with the Duke of Suffolk standing as proxy for the absent groom).

The Maine issue

Suffolk may, during the negotiations at Tours, have offered to trade Maine as an expedient to fix a truce. Subsequently Henry, in the course of personal correspondence with Charles VII, offered to return the district, the effective date of handover to be December 22, 1445. There was no direct military pressure which could account for this retreat. English forces were still tying down Gascony, Anjou, Maine and Normandy. This decision appears to have been dictated by pure appeasement. Consequently, the king did not broadcast his intention and even Suffolk, upon whom the brunt of public opprobrium fell, sought to distance himself from the surrender by issuing a formal disclaimer.

In the event, abandonment of Maine achieved nothing. The incident at Fougères, where an English force sacked the town, merely provided French monarch Charles VII with the pretext he had been seeking to seize Normandy. The increasing burden of taxation imposed by English rule had alienated locals from their ruler, so much so that many Norman towns welcomed their armed countrymen as liberators. Though popular outrage focused on Suffolk, the fault was by no means his alone. The collapse of the English–Burgundian *entente*, the fiscal burden and the king's lack of effective leadership had combined to fatally damage the English position. There would be no recovery.

The end

Indeed, England no longer had the means or the stomach to continue the fight. Subject towns and provinces groaned under harsh and arbitrary rule, and the mounting cost of continuing a losing war was exacerbated by the king's difficulties in controlling his personal finances. Since his marriage, expenditure on the king's household had more than tripled, with Parliament expected to make up the shortfall. Henry had a war he couldn't win and a lifestyle he couldn't afford. The people focused their anger on the king's closest advisors, including Suffolk; all of them came to violent ends.

This situation was made worse by yet more defeats in France. Having regained Normandy at very little cost, Charles VII naturally turned his eyes southwards towards Gascony. The city of Bordeaux was threatened as the French swept through the province, and the castellan agreed to lower his flag should relief not arrive by June 14, 1451. None came and the city surrendered. Three centuries of English domination had come to an end. The loss of Bordeaux constituted a disaster of the first magnitude and there appeared no hope of its recovery. Matters took a temporary turn for the better when, in the autumn, the Earl of Shrewsbury, Shakespeare's Bull Talbot, retook the city. In the summer of 1453, the brief English ascendancy ended for good when Talbot was overwhelmed and killed at Castillon on July 17.

The Hundred Years War had gone on for more than a century. Despite many victories, England had lost its hold on France.

——▶ Profile: Götz von Berlichingen ◀—— (Götz of the Iron Hand)

The splendidly named Götz of the Iron Hand (1480–1562), was a German (Franconian) *Reichsritter* – a gentlemanly name for what was essentially a mercenary. Born in Württemberg, he bought Hornberg Castle in 1517 from the spoils of internecine wars and lived there until his death at the age of 82. As a young man, he'd been employed by Frederick I, Margrave of Brandenburg-Ansbach, and fought for the emperor Maximilian I. He saw plenty of action and built up a reputation that enabled him to form his own mercenary company.

Götz was fighting for the Bavarians in 1504 when he was shot in the hand by an early form of gun. Though the hand had to be amputated, he had two bespoke iron prostheses crafted to use in its place, and these are now on display at Jagsthausen Castle in Germany. The loss of his hand didn't slow Götz down, and when not fighting for wages, he found time to pursue a series of feuds and vendettas. He was at odds with the city of Nuremberg and used this as a pretext to rob a party of merchants in 1512. The emperor was outraged and fined him 14,000 gulden (around $1.75 million in today's money). Götz had also fallen out with the Principality of Mainz – his feud with the prince archbishop of Mainz was one of 15 serious vendettas he conducted during the course of his life – and kidnapped the Count of Waldeck. This resulted in another hefty fine.

In 1519, Götz signed up to fight for the Duke of Wurttemberg, holding the town of Möckmühl against the Swabian League, a defensive alliance between several German states. He was finally starved into surrender and became a prisoner of the burghers of Heilbronn, a town he had pillaged more than once. That cost him another 2,000 gulden (over $200,000 in today's terms).

Götz was not a natural champion of oppressed peasantry, yet, on the outbreak of the German Peasants' War in 1524, he signed up to fight with the rebels. He maintained that this was to control their worst excesses; he failed to do so and soon repented of his allegiance. The electors were not impressed and, after the rebellion was crushed, Götz was called to account for his behavior. He managed to talk his way out of it but his old enemies, the Swabian League (who had long memories and a longer reach) captured him at Augsburg and he was again imprisoned for the next two years.

From 1540, Götz served Charles V, the Holy Roman Emperor, and, two years later, he fought against the Ottoman Turks before turning his attention towards the French. By now he was in his mid-sixties, and finally hung up his sword sometime after. Luckily for historians, Götz wrote his memoirs before he died; Goethe wrote a play about him in 1773 and Jean-Paul Sartre also features him as a character.

CHAPTER 6

GAME OF THRONES

For what is in this world but grief and woe?

Shakespeare: *King Henry VI*, Part 3; Act 2, Scene V

THE WARS OF THE ROSES WERE not, surprisingly, fought over horticulture. The name is in fact a later one, which was first used by Sir Walter Scott in 1829, but has since entered common usage. The series of campaigns fought across England and the Borders in the mid–late 15th century were rather political in nature. Henry VI of England came to the throne in 1422; he was always deeply religious, generally useless and occasionally mad. Richard, Duke of York, felt that he had a better claim to the throne. This was technically true, but York, for most of his career, was content to be the loyal subject, much put upon by the King's jealous advisors, particularly the Duke of Somerset.

To make matters worse, the Hundred Years War with France had ended, and the outcome was unfavorable for the English. The appearance of Joan of Arc – with her direct line to God and her surprising military talent – raised the siege of Orleans and put new heart into the French. From here it was all downhill for the British. Eventually, in 1453, the last English army was defeated at Castillon, signalling the end of over 115 years of conflict. Significant numbers of soldiers were free to return home, but back in England they found themselves unemployed. Eventually the Duke of York, who had subsidised the cost of the French War from his own pocket and who deeply resented goings-on at court, decided to do something about it.

First, a battle was fought in the streets of St Albans, where York disposed of his rival the Duke of Somerset. Another battle was fought at Blore Heath, after which York had to flee the realm. Eventually, his nephew, the Earl of Warwick, called "The Kingmaker," managed a successful comeback, but for York the triumph was very short lived. He was killed in yet another battle, at Wakefield, and his eldest son, the Earl of March, soon to be Edward IV, inherited his claim. Young Edward, with Richard Neville, Earl of Warwick ("The Yorkists"), squared up to Henry's army ("The Lancastrians") at Towton near Tadcaster in North Yorkshire on a cold Easter Sunday. Though not as famous as some of its medieval counterparts, Towton (also known as the battle of Palmsunday Field) was possibly the biggest battle ever fought on English soil; as many as 28,000 men were killed on both sides and the Lancastrians were effectively massacred.

Writing in the *Sunday Times Magazine* in the wet summer of 2008, journalist and writer A. A. Gill visited the field of Towton. He found that

> it would be impossible to walk here and not feel the dread underfoot – the echo of desperate events vibrating just behind the hearing.

Journey into battle

Young Edward dragged his army, massive by the standards of the day, up the long, cold and wet road to Yorkshire, to their first major wet gap crossing over the Don. By Friday, March 27, the Yorkists were drawing close to Ferrybridge and an even greater obstacle. It was imperative to seize this bridgehead over the Aire. John Radcliffe, Lord Fitzwalter, attempted to take the crossing

Engraving by Charles Oliver Murray (1842–1923) of Edward IV (center) during the battle of Towton.

by a bold *coup de main*. It seems clear his assault drove back the defenders, if indeed there were any posted and, though the bridge had been damaged, it was repairable.

John Clifford, 9th Baron, immortalized as the "Butcher" by Shakespeare (he'd supposedly killed Edward's younger brother Edmund, Earl of Rutland, in cold blood at Wakefield), led a surprise counter-attack in the darkness. Lord Fitzwalter was taken by surprise and killed, his survivors driven back. By noon, Richard Neville, Earl of Warwick, who'd been wounded in the fracas, was explaining the debacle to Edward at Pontefract. Edward, having steadied Warwick and others who'd taken fright, launched a series of planned assaults to wrest back the crossing. This was a tactical situation where a few bold, well placed soldiers could hold back an army, so it would not be an easy task. The narrowness of the ground denied Edward any opportunity to bring weight of numbers to bear. Most chroniclers appear to agree that the fighting was hard and costly.

Against such stiff opposition frontal attacks were useless. A bright idea was required, and luckily Edward had one. Warwick was ordered to remain at Ferrybridge and continue pinning Clifford there. The wily Lord Fauconberg, Edward's uncle, would lead a strong flanking movement, through a swollen but passable ford, three miles upstream at Castleford. Clifford might, in turn, be surprised when the Yorkists appeared on his right flank. This seasoned old Yorkist got the better of the Lancastrian lord by springing a rather neat ambush of his own. As the two forces scrapped along the main route north towards Towton, Clifford and his lieutenant Neville may have been confident of their ability to stave off defeat till they reached the safety of their own lines.

What then went so badly wrong for the Lancastrians? It's possible, likely even, that on reaching Ferrybridge and setting off after his opponents, Fauconberg detached a force to ride fast along the old Roman High Road, running parallel and to the west, then swerving through Saxton to block the line of Clifford's retreat at Dintingdale. It was this surprise which finished "the Flower of Craven" (Craven's band of 500 fighting men). At Dinting Dale, the Westmorland men made their final stand. Clifford went down to an archer when, it is said, he injudiciously lifted his bevor (neck guard) to have a drink of water.

With the path cleared, Edward led the bulk of the army toward the crossing over the river at Castleford. By dusk, the Yorkists were safely over the last significant geographical obstacle between them and the Lancastrians. Edward's scouts were as far forward as Saxton, but the heavy baggage was left behind at Ferrybridge. The Yorkist army would be facing a cold and hungry bivouac.

The ground past Towton rises gently to form a low plateau, the slope barely perceptible except to the west, where there is a steep decline into the valley of the Cock Beck. This dale was more densely forested in the 15th century, a tangle of scrub, alder and birch, poorly drained. To the south-west, up beyond the eponymous Palmsunday Field, the rise becomes more noticeable, still topped by the stand of timber named Castle Hill Wood. The swell is neatly bisected by the lateral depression of Towton Dale, which itself slopes into what was, at that time, a marshy gully in the west.

It's generally accepted that the Lancastrians, on the day of the battle, spread along the crown of the ridge line, north of the dale, immediately to the south of the present monument. The Yorkists then had to deploy on the higher ground lying further to the south. Somerset's men might have advanced some 300 meters southwards, leaving Towton Dale behind. The Duke was certainly not blind to the potential for ambush offered by Castle Hill Wood and concealed cavalry there, screened by the trees. The upland landscape stood desolate – a patchwork of small fields and heath at the end of winter; sky close and laden with the promise of yet more snow.

As the Yorkists finally began to filter across at Ferrybridge in late afternoon on March 28, the three main divisions – or "battles" of their army – marched apart, following the old dictum: "march divided, fight united." Cold and apprehension would have prevented many from seeking rest, though others would be so exhausted that sleep came on regardless.

The battle of Towton

Dawn on March 29, Palmsunday; a dank morning, cold, sharp, needle tipped showers were soon falling. To marshal the scattered Yorkist army, dragging men from a few hours fitful rest to ply them with cold rations and small beer for those that had the stomach for it, was a major exercise. As sombre priests moved before assembled companies, men knelt to take a scrap of earth – rather than the usual bread in their mouths. Mortality is a powerful incentive to piety and no medieval soldier would draw weapons before looking to his soul.

As the Yorkists toiled up the slope from Saxton, they'd have stayed out of sight of their enemies deploying on the distant ridge. Having his right flank resting on the edge of the steep decline was an obvious tactic for Somerset. His left reached across the Ferrybridge road toward the other slope, to a point where wet

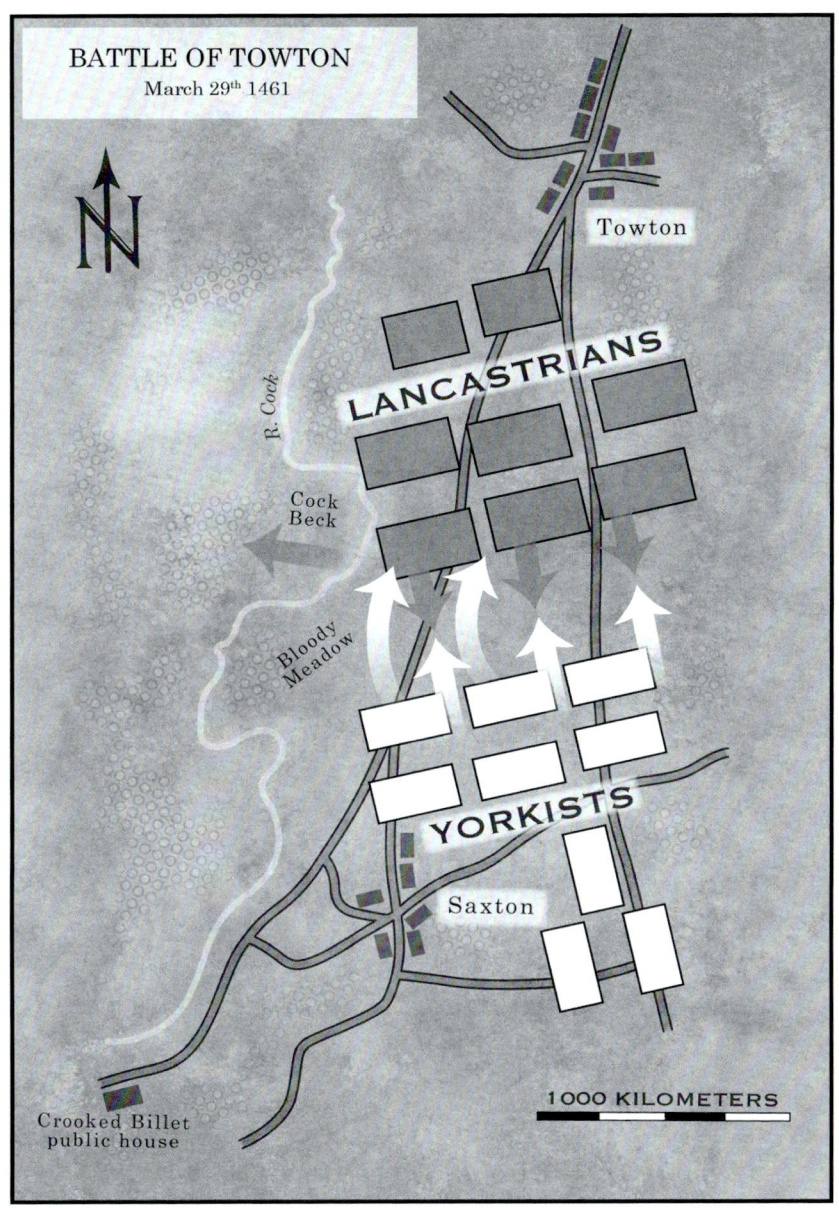

Map 3: The battle of Towton. (Artwork by Chloe Rodham)

ground gave protection. There is debate as to whether the armies mustered in linear formation or in line astern, though it's generally agreed that Fauconberg commanded the Yorkist vanguard – front line – with Warwick in the center and Edward leading the third.

Across Towton Vale, Andrew Trollope and the Earl of Northumberland (who shared command of the Lancastrian Vanguard) took the Lancastrian front or right, though Trollope at some point seems to have led the ambush party. Dacre and Lord Welles held the center, Exeter and Somerset the left. A glance at the map confirms this analysis. To mass men in dense columns bunched into line would have been self-defeating, ranked formations would allow fresh men to be rotated through. An armored man can keep fighting for perhaps 10–15 minutes at best. If we accept the chroniclers view that this battle lasted up to ten hours (or even half that) then clearly such constant refreshment was essential.

From wherever they approached it would not be until the Yorkists had reached the lip of the plateau that they got their

On the field, **panic**, like courage, is collective. Men who have fought bravely may give way once the fear virus spreads. The fear would usually take hold at the rear first. Those at the front are too much occupied with the business of survival to contemplate flight. Once the fear spreads, it rages. As they run, men will cast aside weapons, harness and helmets, too restrictive as they struggle to find breath for flight. The adversary, released from the tension of combat, vision blurred by "the red mist," will have all the opportunity to take out the fleeing, undefended men. In medieval battles where combatants fought primarily on foot, those winning the advantage, seeing their enemies scatter, would have their horses near enough to hand. From then on, it was blood sport.

first glimpse of the Lancastrian army. Even with biting wind and driven flurries, the enemy strength would have been blindingly obvious: silken banners unfurled and harness gleaming, breaks in the sleet showing the massed rows of bills. It was to be a battle, yet also it was a vendetta, a blood feud seeded between noble families across both sides of the dale. All had lost fathers, brothers, cousins and friends. Nobody was expecting any quarter.

The obvious strength of the Lancastrian position may explain why Edward was in no hurry to come to contact. His men were almost certainly outnumbered, with the seriously ill Duke of Norfolk's division still some distance behind. As the ranks were shuffled out into line, between ten and eleven in the morning, a brisk shower of dense rain and sleet gusted over the field, chased by a strong southerly wind. This blew hail directly into the faces of the Lancastrians, obscuring their vision.

Fauconberg, his veteran's eye quick to spot an opportunity, ordered his bowmen to advance and loose, shooting at extreme range but with the scurrying wind to lend wings to their flights; *nock, draw, loose…* Just as smartly they then fell back again. The arrow storm thumped home and the Lancastrians shot in reply, but they just hit empty ground, 40 odd meters short. The cunning old warrior moved up and repeated the process.

Such exchanges of missiles frequently dictated the outcome of a fight, as the losing side had no option but to move up and engage. Arrows would have overwhelmed the Lancastrian ranks and, while a man at arms in full plate might escape injury, anyone less well protected might not. Men were snatched from the ranks to writhe and shudder on the snow, some riddled with shafts, stuck like porcupines through their bodies, limbs and faces. As one volley struck home another was whistling behind. Somerset's problem was his divisions were deployed primarily for defense, attacking would be trickier.

We have no knowledge as to the duration of the archery duel. In all probability it was very short, perhaps not more than ten minutes. If we allow Fauconberg some 10,000 bows shooting at a rate of ten shafts per minute, which a skilled archer could easily achieve, and accept ten minutes' duration then the Yorkists will have shot off nearly a million arrows.

A great shout of "King Henry!" rolled over the windswept ground as the Lancastrians surged forward. The tramp of armored men, slogging over wet slush, drowned the keening of the wind, then there was a great crash as opposing ranks collided. The biggest and bloodiest fight in the history of the British Isles was now fully underway. King Edward had pointedly sent his own horse to the rear, showing he would live or die with his soldiers; such gestures were important and marked Edward as a responsible leader.

Fighting in the mêlée was not confined to men-at-arms. **Archers** could play their part, as they'd shown in earlier battles such as Agincourt in 1415 where they broke ranks to savage French knights stumbling through the mud. Lightly harnessed, strong and agile, these formidable men made deadly opponents wielding sword or falchion and buckler. Two or three would target an armored knight, one would engage his point, the other would aim to hook him behind the knee and bring him down. A dagger thrust to the eye or genitals would finish the job. This was civil war: losers would forfeit their estates so their cash value, in terms of ransoms, was zero. There is a commonly held view that both sides had given an order there should be no quarter. If it was so, this would have added to the terrific fury of the contest.

This was to be the battle for England and the Lancastrian left was the first to engage, Northumberland, on the far flank, lagging behind. Exactly why is uncertain. It's very possible his companies had suffered the most from Fauconberg's barrage and he may have needed more time to order his ranks. Percy's apparent failure on the right to match the momentum of the left would continue to dog Lancastrian deployment on the field. For the whole of their advance the attackers would still be subject to a hail of arrows, men marking targets more closely as the gap narrowed.

With the order to advance, surviving Lancastrian archers would have fallen back upon their main body, commanded ostensibly by Trollope and Northumberland. With last minute adjustments to harness, a final mouthful of water, and doubtless many a quick prayer, the ranks marched on. In such conditions, any advance would be sedate rather than rapid. The line was long and the going treacherous, ground already carpeted with dead and dying from the opening exchanges. Snow was falling steadily now, casting a thickening blanket over corpses.

It was essential for Edward to maintain cohesion. As the Yorkist archers in turn filtered back between companies of their own billmen, the stage was set for a momentous clash of men-at-arms. Until now, both sides had only seen their enemies at a distance. As the Lancastrian army plodded steadily up the slope towards them, the Yorkists would finally see faces, even though so many would be impersonal in closed helmets. Nor were these necessarily strangers: civil war pits brother against brother, father against son.

It's unlikely the Yorkists continued to wait passively. As the bows withdrew, the bills would move forward, seeking momentum of their own; the result, a murderous, hacking mêlée of bills, poleaxes and swords. In such close combat the number of fatal casualties would be perhaps less than might be expected. Greatest loss of life always occurred when one side was in retreat and became easy pickings for their foes. In spite of the terrible losses they had endured, their advance allowed the Lancastrians to shake out their line and bring their greater weight of numbers to bear. For Edward, there was no sign of Norfolk and his much-needed reinforcements.

As the mêlée erupted, many suffered from cuts to the head, body and lower limbs. If a man fell, he was lost, snuffed out by a flurry of blows. The noise would have been terrific, a cacophony of grinding blades, shouts, exhortations, curses, and screams of injured and dying men. The mounds of dead would have built up steadily. This was not a neat Hollywood-style coming together of opposing lines. Knots of men would eddy and, temporarily disengage as ranks were thinned or disordered. The press of dead men would form a considerable barrier so that the living would have to fight over the heaps. In the dense fog of battle men would stand with comrades in their companies. Telling who was friend and who was foe wasn't always easy, and in some Wars of the Roses battles – such as Barnet in 1471 – confusion would breed disaster.

If the Yorkists enjoyed the considerable morale booster of having an inspiring and youthful king on the field, they still lacked numbers. As the fight ground on, this began to tell. The Lancastrians were steadily gaining ground. At one point Edward was saved by the swift action of a Welsh retainer, Daffyd ap Matthew. In recognition of this, the King granted his savior the honor of standard bearer and the insertion of "Towton" into his family arms. Edward might have been inclined to indolence and hedonism off the field, but on it he was active and intelligent.

We cannot now fully understand, nor perhaps even imagine, the nature of close medieval combat. Most contemporary military actions come no closer than perhaps a couple of hundred yards. Even in 20th and 21st century eyewitness accounts of battle, participants gain only a limited and often distorted view of events around them. In the heat of battle, with adrenaline pumping and the senses deafened by sound, it is highly unlikely any individual would have any glimmer of wider understanding. The business of staying alive tends to be fairly pressing.

Ambush

By mid-afternoon the attrition was beginning to tell in Somerset's favor as the Yorkists began to appear increasingly beleaguered, and he might just have chosen this crucial moment to spring an ambush from Castle Hill Wood. The blow fell on the left of the Yorkist line. Evidence for this is largely anecdotal, but the lie of the ground was well suited to such a move, and the frequent snow showers would act as a further screen. If an attack of this nature could be successfully launched, the Yorkists would find themselves being struck on both flanks. The Lancastrians had likely stayed mounted and the charge had enough momentum to push the Yorkist left flank down the line of the present B1217. Part of the army may even have broken, provoking a crisis for the young king and his senior officers.

Many historians believe that the ambush party was led by Trollope and Lord Rivers, Edward's future father-in-law. Castle Hill Wood is – and was – dense and tangled; it wouldn't be possible to conceal a large force of mounted men-at-arms actually under the trees, much less launch a cohesive charge. The ambush party would have to have been concealed in the lee of the wood but where they would still have been invisible to the Yorkists. That complete surprise was possible seems underlined by the fact there is no suggestion in any of the chronicles that the Yorkists tried to anchor their flank by occupying the hill. The potential for ambush seems to have been overlooked; this failure could have cost Edward the battle.

Trollope is credited with being the architect of the ruse that destroyed Richard of York and Richard Neville, Earl of Salisbury at Wakefield. If such a tactic could be recycled at Towton the results might be equally spectacular. If we accept the ambush developed as suggested, Edward would have to shuffle any final reserves together with his household men to contain the breach. These measures clearly worked as the line did not fold. The very size of his army helped; for a smaller force, as was the case with Hotspur at Otterburn over 70 years before, the shock of contact could roll up an army and lead inevitably to defeat. At Towton, though Edward sustained casualties and sections of his third line fled, the line just about held.

The final outcome of the battle still hung in the balance, but the advantage shifted inexorably to the more numerous Lancastrians. Edward may have been saved from a worse catastrophe by possible command and control failures, such as Northumberland pushing on too slowly to capitalize on the partial success of the ambush party. Indeed, his division may have been forced to give ground with the Earl himself, at this critical point, being struck down. This would now result in the contending battle lines assuming the shape of a shallow "V" with the apex just east of the Towton road. Northumberland's apparent failure to exploit Trollope's stroke appears, at first sight, inexplicable. Cowardice was not a Percy characteristic, Northumberland's father, grandfather and great-grandfather had all died *with harness on their backs.*

If the Earl was injured at around this time (he was to die of his wounds), then his wing may have lost momentum or, quite possibly, the fog of war and appalling weather frustrated coordination. In any event, Percy's failure was York's salvation. Had the whole line pushed forward, the Yorkist position would have been even graver.

If the Earl of Northumberland had indeed been laid low at this point, his affinity (his followers and those connected to him) would lose heart. This may have given the Yorkists on that wing a break and allowed them not only to stabilize their position, but to win some measure of ground, pushing their opponents back and deepening the angle of the "V."

Lord Dacre of Gilsland (of a famously aggressive Cumbrian family) was also amongst the casualties. Like Clifford, overcome with thirst, he removed his sallet only to be transfixed by an arrow. Legend insists he fell to a crossbow bolt shot by a youthful sniper carefully concealed in a bur (elderberry) tree. Dehydration and suffocating heat, trapped within a steel carapace, can be as debilitating as wounds. Dacre probably died in North Acres but, despite this loss of another senior officer, the Lancastrians pressed on, forcing the Yorkists to give ground.

A clue as to why Trollope's ambush wasn't decisive may lie in Waurin's description; he refers to the fleeing Yorkists being "chased for about eleven miles." This is reminiscent of other battles where cavalry commanders failed to rally their riders after the initial tactical advantage had been won, frittering away the fruits of victory. We may imagine the experienced Trollope fuming at the indiscipline of Rivers' marchers as they fixed their eyes firmly on loot and dashed off in headlong pursuit. If so, this may have saved Edward.

The knife-edge

Yet Edward's situation was still critical. All of the Yorkist reserves, under Wenlock and Dinham, would have been committed. The young king's men were steadily pushed back toward the lip of the escarpment; the Yorkists had been shaken and depleted on

The battle of Hexham (May 15, 1464) was fought near the town of Hexham in Northumberland and marked the end of significant Lancastrian resistance in the north. John Neville led a modest force of 3,000–4,000 men, and routed the Lancastrians. Most of the rebel leaders were captured and executed, including Henry Beaufort, Duke of Somerset, and Lord Hungerford. Henry VI, however, was kept safely away for a change and escaped to the north.

the left even if they had more than held their own on the right. As the left stumbled, the right would have to conform (adjust their position so that they balanced the other wing) and, in so doing, surrender the momentum they'd managed to build up so far. If the Lancastrians could maintain their steady, unrelenting pressure, they'd sweep their battered enemies clear off the plateau and King Henry VI, safe in York, would be firmly back on his throne.

Edward, his Black Bull banner streaming in the wind, was the epitome of knighthood, an inspiration to his bone-weary soldiers. George Neville, the Kingmaker's brother and admittedly partisan, refers in his memoirs to the courage and leadership of not only the king, but of his brother, Richard of Gloucester and uncle, Lord de Fauconbridge. Personal leadership was the vital element of medieval generalship. Edward of York perfectly filled this role, his great height, commanding physique, charisma and personal courage embodying the chivalric ideal.

Joan of Arc on horseback in an illustration from the 1504 manuscript Les vies des femmes célèbres, *by Antoine Dufour.*

Edward's skills would be needed more than ever at this critical juncture on the bare upland plateau of Towton. But where was Norfolk? His arrival was now crucial to Yorkist survival. Without fresh men to redress the balance, defeat appeared inevitable. We can only speculate why the Duke's progress was so slow and it seems reasonable to suppose his deteriorating health was a factor.

Locked like punch-drunk fighters in a

deadly embrace, the armies eddied and swayed on the southern rim. Somerset might have felt the scent of victory in his nostrils. One last sustained effort would sweep the Yorkists into chaos and oblivion. Edward and his household men would be shoring up the line wherever a fracture seemed imminent but the Yorkists would sense that time was running out. Without Norfolk, they appeared doomed.

Norfolk to the rescue

Desperately ill, the exhausted duke may have been at Pontefract on the evening of March 28. Nonetheless, he had his men on the move next morning, though whether he was at their head is uncertain. Following the old London road through Sherburn-in-Elmet, past the corpse strewn field at Dintingdale where the stiffening remains of the dead stayed frozen in the sack-like postures of death, it's possible his division encountered fugitives from the rout sparked by Trollope's ambushers. At some point during the afternoon Norfolk's troops began arriving on the field, deploying on their comrades' right flank. Their much-needed and fresh reinforcements were able to both prop up the faltering Yorkist line and provide greater parity of numbers.

As these companies mustered at the base of the plateau, the carnage above them would have been hidden, though the noise would have been deafening. That Norfolk's men deployed on the extreme flank of Edward's right was more accidental than planned: it was on this flank that the Yorkists had won something of an edge. The relief enabled surviving Yorkist officers to extend past and overlap the opposition. Moreover, this came at a time when those who had been battling so desperately for several hours were utterly exhausted. If we assume the archery duel opened hostilities between 10 am and 11 am, and time Norfolk's arrival for around 2 pm to 3 pm, with the final Lancastrian collapse occurring an hour later, this is a fight of around five hours, still a prodigious span.

Somerset moved men to shore up his left while trying to maintain pressure on Edward's center and right. For the moment, the adversaries were equally matched. Fighting continued deep into the wet afternoon, scudding cloud driven by the sharp-edged wind, scattering of hail and snow blinding the combatants and settling a pall over the rising mounds of dead and wounded. Nonetheless, the providential arrival of Norfolk's division may finally have been the decisive factor. When the fighting was of such long duration and the mettle of the parties so finely balanced, any fresh reinforcement at the crisis point must have exercised a significant effect. Somerset had been within an ace of winning the battle when his ambush party crashed against the Yorkist left. Yet Norfolk's reinforcement, albeit less dramatic, may have achieved a greater tactical advantage.

The battle of Bosworth: Henry Tudor, backed by French money, landed at Milford Haven in August 1485 with a force of 500 followers and about 1500 French soldiers. He won the support of the most influential landowner in South Wales together with his stepfather Lord Stanley (whose eldest son was being held prisoner by Richard III as an insurance of good behavior.

Richard III initially did nothing about the invasion as he assumed the Welsh landowners would see Henry as a threat and group their forces against him. By the time he realized his mistake, Henry was in Leicestershire. Richard moved to block him, encountering his opponent two-and-a-half miles south of Market Bosworth.

Those struggling in the frenzy would have little sense of events beyond their immediate periphery. Pouring with sweat in clammy harness, vision restricted to the narrow opening of the visor, disorientated by a constant, relentless crescendo of noise, it would be impossible to gain a meaningful insight into the shifting fortunes of the armies. But the Yorkists had stopped retreating. It was now their turn to push forward. Pressure from Norfolk's fresh units was causing Somerset's line to bend backwards in response, curving like a flexed bow, still in good order.

At some point in the long, blood-soaked afternoon, the Lancastrians began to give way; at first, a trickle that swelled into a stream, then a river, finally a flood. How and precisely when this occurred we can't say, probably late afternoon. Even with Norfolk's men deploying on the right flank of the Yorkist line and the consequential pressure exerted against the Lancastrian left there was no immediate collapse. Both sides had sustained heavy casualties and these would likely have fallen heaviest upon officers on both sides. Lord Scrope, Sir Edward Jenny and the Kentishman Horne were down on the Yorkist side; Northumberland and Dacre certainly, Trollope perhaps, from the Lancastrians.

It's possible the men on King Henry's right began to waver. The line did not fold but must have given ground, back over the corpse-infested mire of blood-fed slush, a withdrawal, fairly steady, over space so dearly bought. Maybe there was another of those pauses as survivors shook themselves into formations and newcomers were fully integrated.

Stalemate was something Edward could not afford – it was time for one last push. Few men of his age have ever faced so great a challenge and risen so magnificently. If we really want to know why the Yorkists won, it has to be down to superior leadership. Edward was the perfect fusion of knight and general, Lancelot and Longshanks in one.

Edward, alongside Warwick the Kingmaker, drove his men forward, ordered their lines and by personal example and exhortation led them on for the final, critical push. Norfolk's arrival, however belated, gave them the boost they needed. Sir James Ramsay makes the sour but true observation:

Henry's presence usually entailed failure wherever he went.

Somerset was not cast in the same mold as his adversary. His command style had been competent but uninspired. He had neither the majesty of kingship nor the Homeric bravura needed. Put simply, Edward was the better man.

Once morale was gone, rout was inevitable, the collapse finally swift and terrifyingly sudden as the thinning ranks at the front found themselves deserted. Polydore Vergil, chronicler for Henry VII, wrote a record of the battle. His account, though it postdates the battle by half a century, does suggest that the collapse, when it came, was swift.

Now the killing could really begin.

The battle of Rouvray, February 12, 1429: Also known as "**the battle of the Herrings**." Commanded by Sir John Fastolf, a convoy of 300 wagons carrying supplies for the English besiegers of Orleans was attacked near the town of Rouvray by the French and their Scottish allies.

Deploying his wagons as an improvised fortification (including those with barrels of herrings on them) Fastolf fought off the enemy.

Slaughter on Bloody Meadow

It was by the rim of Towton Dale that the Lancastrian line had finally fractured. A few hardy souls determined to form rally points around their banners and sell their lives as dearly as possible, but most just joined the deluge. Many scrambled or slid down the slush-covered gradient toward Cock Beck. The site that was to become known as Bloody Meadow became a vast killing field.

Panicking survivors fought each other to cross the narrow span of the bridge, swirling waters below swollen with the frequent downpours. Exhausted men were dragged down by the weight of harness and sodden jacks. It was said the waters were so bloated with the tide of corpses men could cross dry shod over a "bridge of bodies." As survivors pelted through the narrow lanes of Towton and on to Tadcaster, they were harried and hacked by swirling knots of cavalry who carried the slaughter virtually to the gates of York. Nobody wanted to open their doors.

As writer A. A. Gill pointed out, Towton, for all its magnitude and drama, plays a poor relation to other more renowned fields such as Hastings, Bosworth or Culloden. Most people remember the tale of Harold and the arrow in 1066 from school history class. Partisans and detractors of that most enigmatic of Yorkists and controversial of monarchs, Richard III, have kept the memory of Bosworth alive and still happily contentious. However, thanks to the efforts of the Towton Battlefield Society, there is much new interpretation and a first-class battlefield trail now in place.

From this point, the axis of the war shifted north to Northumberland, where the Lancastrians still held the northern castles and poor, pathetic King Henry, largely without a kingdom, held a court of sorts at Bamburgh.

Even after the disaster at Hexham, a few diehard Lancastrians continued to hold out at Bamburgh, forcing Warwick to unleash his siege guns. He was particularly annoyed, not just because it was a lot of extra trouble and expense, but also because he ran the risk of damaging the valuable castle. He warned the defenders that for every stone dislodged by the bombardment, he'd take off one of their heads. Not surprisingly, when the Lancastrian commander was knocked out cold by falling masonry, his men took the opportunity to surrender.

Richard

Richard, Duke of Gloucester has not enjoyed a good press, despite the efforts of many down the centuries who have argued for a more balanced and nuanced approach. He was to seize the throne and rule for two turbulent years until defeated and killed by Henry Tudor at Bosworth. He's most famous as the alleged murderer of his two nephews, the "princes in the tower." Whether or not Richard was involved in the deaths is still a hot topic of debate among historians. We do know that Richard's short, dark and violent reign came to a suitably dramatic end at the battle of Bosworth on August 22, 1485, the date that traditionally marks the end of the Middle Ages. But, in fact, the Tudor period would not begin for some time, as Henry Tudor had to fight for his throne again two years later on Stoke Field, perhaps a more accurate cut-off point for the Middle Ages.

You could say it marked the end of the cult of chivalry as well. The cult and its resonances would continue to reverberate but the bell of history was already tolling. In 1494, the French and Spanish would square up for the Great Wars in Italy and these would be different. Mass armies would be dominated by mercenary pikemen and latterly by hand-held firearms – not good for gentlemen. And as for all that fine very expensive harness, it would be relegated to the tournament. As Kipling said centuries later:

two thousand pounds of education drops to a ten-rupee *jezail* [Afghan rifle].

➤➤ Profile: Joan of Arc ➤➤

Joan of Arc, perhaps the most famous French commander of all time, has permeated Western culture and become synonymous with medieval warfare and charismatic leadership. But how did a teenage girl from the province of Lorraine earn her place in history? A combination of the need for a national myth and of her own personal qualities, most likely. Joan embodied most of the knightly virtues – courage, piety, loyalty and self-sacrifice – even if she was actually sacrificed by an unfortunate combination of English vindictiveness and a cynical French monarchy.

Jeanne d'Arc (*c.* 1412–1431), known also as the "Maid of Orleans" and "La Pucelle," was born to a prosperous farming family at Domremy, north-east France. At this time, during the so-called "Lancastrian" phase of the Hundred Years War, the English appeared to be doing rather well. Henry V was dead, but his capable brother, the Earl of Bedford was continuing the fight in the name of the young Henry VI, whom England viewed as the rightful king of France. Henry VI's mother was a French princess, though his principal inheritance was the Valois instability rather than any practical source of aid or support from the French crown. But the French seemed incapable of beating any kind of English army, no matter how small.

Joan had other ideas. She believed she heard voices – and not just any voices, but Archangel Gabriel and the saints Margaret and Catherine. This was a dangerous claim in and of itself, as the distinction between mystic and heretic could be awfully blurred. But Joan was nothing if not determined, and she clearly had a very potent charisma that inspired all who met her despite her youth, gender and socio-economic status.

The uncrowned Charles VII of France needed a miracle: Paris had fallen and the Earl of Salisbury was laying siege to Orleans; Charles's attempt at sending a relief force had been seen off by

Sir John Fastolf, who fought the aptly named "Battle of the Herrings" at Rouvray.

It was Joan who marched to Orleans at the head of the Dauphin's army and lifted the siege. No sooner had she done that than she beat Fastolf and Bull Talbot both together during the battle of Patay on June 18, 1429, where each commander blamed the other for their defeat. This proved to be a tipping point in the war: from this point on, the English would taste only the bitter bile of defeat and all their precious bastions would fall over the next 20 years. Joan's successes enabled Charles's full coronation at Reims. It might have been easier for Joan if she'd died at Orleans; falling in your hour of glory has much to recommend it, especially when surviving means being captured by the Burgundians, then allies of England. Joan was sold on to the Earl of Warwick and put on trial by an ecclesiastical court headed up by the turncoat Frenchman, the Bishop of Beauvais.

There was never much doubt over the outcome of the trial: Joan was convicted of heresy. Though she confessed, she tore up her statement and went defiantly to the stake on May 30, 1431, already long written-off by her king, who'd refused to pay any ransom. She was probably 19 years old. Militarily it didn't matter; a new generation of savvy French captains were on the up. Politically, however, it was totally self-defeating. Far from being regarded as a heretic, she became an instant martyr, and her memory would haunt the English clear out of France.

Soon it was official: The Pope authorized an enquiry barely a generation after Joan's immolation and all charges were dismissed. She was *officially* a martyr now. Napoleon elevated her to the status of national icon in 1803; just over a century later, she was beatified and finally canonized in 1920. Joan also scored pretty highly in the fictional stakes, Shaw's play *Saint Joan* has never gone out of vogue completely, and there's been a slew of films, books and television shows from the sublime to the ridiculous, ever since. What Joan would have made of Milla Jovovitch, one can only imagine.

CHAPTER 7

IVANHOE

Green Flodden! on thy blood-stain'd head
Descend no rain nor vernal dew;
But still thou charnel of the dead,
May whitening bones thy surface strew!

J. Leyden

19th-century revival

IN THE ENTRANCE HALL TO WINDSOR Castle stands a magnificent Gothic suit of armor for a mounted knight, just the sort of kit you would have expected Richard III to turn up for Bosworth in. But it's just a replica, made and assembled not for battle but for a 19th-century romantic revival, the Eglinton Tournament of 1839. Blame Sir Walter Scott: his novels such as *Ivanhoe* sold in prodigious quantities, the quality pulp fiction of their day – he really reinvented chivalry.

On a rather wet Friday in August 1839, Archibald, Earl of Eglinton held the mock tourney at his appropriately gothic fantasy castle in Ayrshire. It was a society event; the revived cult of chivalry was all the rage. Gentlemen, otherwise under-employed, lined up to take part, including Prince Louis Napoleon, future emperor of the French. The event drew in a crowd of over 100,000, though heavy and persistent showers significantly dampened proceedings. Eglinton lost money but many others did well out of sales of kit and memorabilia. Even if not a success on the day, the tournament spearheaded the massive 19th-century mania for knights and chivalry.

King Arthur

King Arthur and the Knights of the Round Table weren't just a Victorian obsession. The legends surrounding England's late Roman warlord – or *Dux* – had long fascinated us. Geoffrey of Monmouth in his *History of the Kings of Britain* (written *c.* 1130–1140) wrote about Arthur. Roger Mortimer, having unseated Edward II and run off with his Queen, Isabella, postured as Arthur in one of his grand tournaments; a pretension that seems to have confirmed his stepson Edward III's intention to be rid of them both.

Sir Thomas Malory's *Le Morte d'Arthur* hit the shelves in 1485 and has been on them ever since, even though the author himself appears pretty disreputable. Henry VIII, a lover of chivalry (unless you crossed him or had the misfortune to be married to him), had the legendary round table hanging in Winchester castle re-painted for Charles V's official visit in 1522. Oddly, the refreshed image of King Arthur looks a lot like Henry. The table was long thought or hoped to be the original if indeed it ever existed. In fact, dendrochronology has revealed it was probably crafted in Longshanks' day.

Both authors read and marvelled at Roger Llancelyn Green's *King Arthur* published by Puffin. Green was a friend of Tolkien and you can see the likenesses in their writing styles. John Boorman's magisterial *Excalibur* from 1981 with Nigel Terry and Nicol Williamson re-defined Arthur for the late 20th century, while Antoine Fuqua and Guy Ritchie's respective offerings in 2004 and 2017 introduced him to a new generation.

Truth be told, we don't even know if Arthur existed. Myths abound, but historical evidence is sparse. Chronicle references are of a much later date. He is, of course, associated with Tintagel and South Cadbury, but there are many sites in the North of England that also lay claim to an Arthurian connection, including Sewingshields Crags in Northumberland and Birdoswald Fort near Greenhead, the latter possibly *Camboglanna* in Latin – a contender for the last battle of Camlann. Unlikely perhaps, yet the fort clearly shows traces of partial reconstruction and rebuilding in the right period. The battle of Arthuret (*c*. 573 CE) was fought not far away and the wizard Merlin features in the stories about it.

The death of chivalry

On a wet, late summer afternoon in 1513, the army of King James IV of Scotland swept down from Branxton Edge in Northumberland to smash, like a steel-tipped avalanche, into the forces of King Henry VIII, the Scottish king's brother-in-law. Henry wasn't there – he was playing at war in France – but his resumption of the rivalry of the Hundred Years War had prompted James, as an ally of the French, to launch a major diversion against England. His wiser nobles weren't so keen. In the past, such affronts had been met with destructive arrow storms. But this was to be a new type of campaign. James would put his faith in continental infantry tactics, massed phalanxes of pikemen, reminiscent of Alexander's Macedonians. In Europe, the mercenary Swiss were the accepted masters of combat. They fought for cash and employed discipline, cohesion and skill to win battles. They won rather a lot. Charles the Bold of Burgundy, a quixotic product of the chivalric tradition, had found out just how well these tactics worked, when they did for him and his army at Nancy in 1477. Charles's frozen, hacked, mutilated and barely recognizable body was dragged from the river a couple of days later.

More so than the longbow, this was the death knell for chivalry. An age of mass armies was dawning. James tried hard in 1513, drilling his Scottish "foot loons" in the arts of the *puissant* pike rather than their conventional spears. He had guns too, lots of them; a superlative world-class siege train that battered defiant Norham into submission in just five days. Ironically, on the day of battle it was an outmoded, Northern English army, no different from their fathers who'd fought at Bosworth which triumphed. They had guns too, light, handy field pieces that won the opening gun duel against the more cumbersome Scottish ordnance. The battle, which would rage for up to four hours, was decided in the first ten minutes. Unfavorable ground defeated the Scottish pikes before they even came to contact. English bills did the rest. The cull amongst the Scottish gentry was biblical. Like Charles the Bold, James was slashed down in the mêlée and his mangled corpse recovered by the English next day.

Bigger wars needed bigger armies. Knights took too long to train and were too expensive. Their natural independence of spirit, their unwillingness to follow orders, marked them as warriors, not soldiers. Kings needed men who just got on with the job. The introduction of hand-held firearms came at a time when armor was reaching technical perfection, a fusion of practicality with aesthetic perfection, elegant but not unfortunately shot-proof. Even the great Swiss pikes were winnowed by musketry at Biococca less than a decade after Flodden. Another generation of Scottish pikemen went the same way at Pinkie in 1547, stalled by cavalry then shot to pieces by withering volleys. These early firearms were wildly inaccurate and unreliable but they were cheap to manufacture and you could drill a musketeer in a morning. He didn't need a long apprenticeship. Big guns had rendered obsolete the use of the medieval castle as a lord or knight's refuge. Medieval walls could never withstand artillery and siege trains were so expensive they had become solely the tools of princes. In a new age of deepening autocracy, rulers were no longer *primus inter pares* – they ruled increasingly not just as God's anointed but directly by divine right. Gentlemen still mattered; tournaments continued throughout the 16th century and armies would normally be officered by those suited to command by birth rather than purely on merit. Armies of the English Civil Wars (misnamed, as these conflicts affected every part of Great Britain) were, on all sides, initially officered by men of rank. As the wars progressed, those of the middling sort – Fairfax, Cromwell, Waller and Hopkins – would acquire status. The old order, if by no means dispossessed, would be badly dented.

If the idea of knighthood disappeared into history, the lure of chivalry lived on. An officer corps was expected to behave like gentlemen. In Tony Richardson's 1968 film of *The Charge of the Light Brigade*, Sir John Gielgud, playing Lord Raglan, bemoans:

> officers who know too well what they do, such professionalism smacks of murder.

This is romanticized, but the lure of chivalry cast a pall over the British army for generations; knighthood and the officer caste were inextricably linked. It took the new 20th-century concept of industrial war to blow away the traces.

Like King Arthur, the mystique has never faded. Perhaps it never will.

——◆— Profile: Ivanhoe —◆——

While Walter Scott gave us the fictional knight Ivanhoe, it was late 1950s' television that cast Roger Moore in the role and latterly, in 1997, Steven Waddington. The chivalric hero remains evergreen, and his story ever more so:

Wilfred of Ivanhoe is passed over by Cedric of Rotherwood, his Saxon father, for the twin sins of following the Angevin Lionheart and for casting lustful eyes on the ward for whom he has dynastic plans. The Templars (in general) and Sir Brian de

Bois-Guilbert (in particular) are the baddies who, while enjoying Cedric's hospitality, plan to abduct the Jewish merchant Isaac of York. Isaac has a beautiful and feisty daughter, Rebecca.

The scene shifts to a tournament, where an unknown knight bests the swaggering Templars, including de Bois-Guilbert. Prince John is presiding and the mystery jouster nominates Cedric's comely ward Rowena as Belle of the Tournament. On the second day, there's a general mêlée and the plucky knight finds himself surrounded by nasty Normans seeking revenge. He's saved from a sticky end by another unknown paladin, the Black Knight, but, having finally won, he is obliged to reveal he is indeed Wilfred of Ivanhoe returned from the Crusades.

This is now officially a bad day for Prince John, as Ivanhoe's return presages that of his own brother, the rightful king. John "Lackland" has quite got used to sitting on the throne and is none too keen to hand it back. Ivanhoe is laid out by his wounds and requires the capable ministrations of the talented Rebecca to pull through. Isaac is persuaded to transport the injured hero back to York. It's not been a good weekend for the Normans though and, just to cap it all, the archer Robin of Locksley sweeps the board at the butts.

Isaac, Rebecca, Rowena and Cedric, together with the injured Ivanhoe, are all captured in the forest by one of De Bois-Guilbert's henchmen, Front-de-Boeuf, and taken to his castle. Alerted by an escapee, Robin and his merry men attack the robber baron's stronghold. Meanwhile de Bois-Guilbert, despite his rabid anti-Semitism, is entranced by Rebecca, with whom he becomes infatuated, though she rejects his advances. Armed with some handy inside information, the Sherwood men storm the walls, assisted by the Black Knight who reveals himself as none other than King Richard. Front-de-Boeuf is killed but de Bois-Guilbert gets away (still hanging on to Rebecca, whom he drags off into the nearest Templar preceptor).

This was not a well-thought-out plan. The Templar Grand Master decides to try Rebecca as a witch, and de Bois-Guilbert urges her to opt for trial by combat – he'll be her champion. The Grand Master is wise to this and orders de Bois-Guilbert to fight against any champion who appears. Meanwhile, King Richard has achieved a reconciliation between Ivanhoe and his father, and secured him Rowena's hand in marriage. Now fully recovered, Ivanhoe naturally elects to stand as Rebecca's champion. He beats de Bois-Gilbert but spares his life – a noble gesture yet ultimately a worthless one, as the templar dies anyway and Rebecca is safe. She and her father leave England for Spain and Ivanhoe marries Rowena, leaving us wondering if he chose the right girl after all...

Ivanhoe sold at a phenomenal rate. Within less than two weeks, the entire first printing of 10,000 copies was exhausted and the demand for more copies put the printers under serious pressure. Translated into numerous languages, it moved Scott into an international market and can be said to mark the birth of the historical novel.

Yet even then there were those who suggested Rowena was insipid. It's a complaint which has even greater resonance today. Opinion on Rebecca is more mixed: some maintain she is the obvious choice for Ivanhoe whilst others insist he is not good enough for her.

GLOSSARY

Affinity   A magnate's following, comprising not just his own *vassals* or tenants but his friends and allies.

Banneret   A knight who was entitled to carry his own banner, conferred status over more junior knights, more likely to be given a command in battle.

Bevor   A section of plate armor, worn with the *sallet* form of helmet to provide protection to the neck and lower face.

Bill   A pole arm, a deadly fusion of agricultural implement and spear, with a curved axe type blade, a spike for thrusting and a hook on the reverse, a formidable weapon in trained hands.

Bombard   A heavy siege gun of the 15th century, irregular in caliber but throwing a massive ball, perhaps up to 60 pounds (30 kg) in weight.

Captain   The officer responsible for a particular place or location but whose authority was limited to his charge.

Centenar   An officer commanding 100 men.

Chevauchée   A large-scale foray aimed at laying waste the territory of an enemy, to belittle the foe and perhaps force him to accept battle.

Destrier   A warhorse, much prized and of considerable value.

Feudalism   The system of government and land holding introduced into England by William I. Under the feudal pyramid, land was parcelled out to the tenants-in-chief, together with rights attaching thereto, in return for a complex raft of obligations, inherent amongst which was military service for defined periods and duration.

Gorget   Plate armor designed to protect the neck area.

Halberd   A polearm with a broad axe blade.

Hand-and-a-half sword   The knightly sword of the 15th century, often known as a "bastard sword": long, tapering double edged blade, used either for the thrust or the cut.

Harness   Full plate armor.

Hobiler/hobilar   Lightly mounted cavalry or mounted infantry, associated with the light horse of the Anglo-Scottish border.

Jack	A form of protective doublet, stuffed with rags and generally sleeveless, worn by the commons a more sophisticated form was the *brigandine* which had metal plates sewn between the facing and lining so that only the rivet heads, in decorative patterns showed through the fabric covering.
Kettle hat	A form of iron headgear worn by men-at-arms, with a wide protective brim, similar in appearance to British "tin hat" helmets of both world wars.
Lance	A tactical unit built around a knight's following, which could therefore vary in size. Also a long-handled weapon.
Livery	The distinctive coat ("livery coat") worn by a lord's retainers, bearing his badge, hence the expression "livery and maintenance" – the retainer is clothed and fed by his employer in return, in effect, for wearing his private uniform (and assuming his private quarrels). The Battle of Empingham or "Losecote Field" refers to the haste with which the panicked rebels cast off the incriminating livery coats of the erstwhile paymasters Warwick and Clarence.
March	A frontier territory, administered by a warden, "Marcher" lords were those who held lands along the Anglo-Scottish or -Welsh borders.
Poleaxe	A polearm, favored by knights for close quarter combat, an axe blade, spear head and a hammer for battering an armored opponent.
Rondel dagger	A 15th-century, long-bladed knife, carried by all classes, could be used as a weapon or implement.
Sallet	A 15th-century helmet with a swept neckguard and often fitted with a fixed or moveable visor, worn above the *bevor*.
Tenants-in-chief	Magnates who held their lands directly from the Crown, rather than from a superior lord (these were known as sub-tenants).
Vassal	One who holds his land from his feudal superior on terms which involve an obligation of service as a condition of his tenancy.
Vintenar	A type of NCO in charge of a platoon of 20 men.

FOR MORE INFORMATION

The Houston Museum of Natural Science

5555 Hermann Park Drive

Houston, TX 77030

(713) 639-4629

Website: www.hmns.org

Facebook: @natural.science

Twitter: @hmns

YouTube: HMNS - Houston Museum of Natural Science

The Houston Museum of Natural Science is a major learning center and one of the most attended museums in the United States. In the past, it featured an exhibition on knights. Information on this exhibit can be found on the museum's website at: www.hmns.org/exhibits/past-exhibitions/knights.

The Metropolitan Museum of Art

1000 Fifth Avenue

New York, NY 10028

(212) 535-7710

Website: www.metmuseum.org

Facebook and Twitter: @metmuseum

YouTube: The Met

The Metropolitan Museum of Art, known as the Met for short, showcases art from all over the world from as far back as 5,000 years. The museum's collection includes pieces from the time of the knights. Additionally, the website offers a timeline of art history that features information about knights in medieval Europe and different kinds of armor.

The Morgan Library & Museum

225 Madison Avenue

New York, NY 10016

(212) 685-0008

Website: www.themorgan.org

Facebook and Twitter: @morganlibrary

YouTube: The Morgan Library & Museum

The Morgan Library & Museum showcases collections including manuscripts, rare books and ancient works of art. Among these collections are medieval & Renaissance manuscripts and other works having to do with knights.

Worcester Art Museum

55 Salisbury Street

Worcester, MA 01609

(508) 799-4406

Website: www.worcesterart.org

Facebook: @WorcesterArtMuseum

Twitter: @WorcesterArt

The Worcester Art Museum's mission is to "connect people, communities, and cultures through the experience of art." Its collection of arms and armor is the second largest of its kind in the Americas. The museum is also well known for its medieval galleries.

FOR FURTHER READING

INTRODUCTION

We have relied on accepted classics among secondary sources including Sir Charles Oman, Colonel A. H. Burne (both *Battlefields* and *More Battlefields*), Professor Prestwich's *Armies & Warfare in the Middle Ages*, and Andrew Boardman's *The Medieval Soldier in the Wars of the Roses*. The quote from Homer is from W. H. D. Rouse's translation (1964). *There were many rich caparisons ...* is quoted in Prestwich, (p. 178). *What a joyous thing is war ...* is quoted in Boardman, (p. 173). *Because of the said wars ...* is quoted on p. 289 of Peter Traquair's *Freedom's Sword* (London, 1998). Details of the Towton archaeology are from *Blood Red Roses* by Veronica Fiorato and Anthea Boylston (Oxbow 2007).

CHAPTER 1

For Hastings and 1066, we've relied on Marc Morris's *The Norman Invasion* (Windmill 2013). For the origins and development of knighthood we've used Henry Treece and Ewart Oakeshott's *Fighting Men* (Brockhampton Press 1963) and Oakeshott's quartet, *A Knight and His Weapons/His Horse/His Armour/His Castle*. Another survivor is Frederick Wilkinson's *Arms & Armour* (Black 1963). We've also used Marc Morris's *Castle* (Windmill 2012), B. R. Lewis's *Life in a Medieval Castle*, *Castles & Context* by R. Liddiard (Windgather Press 2005), *Medieval Fortifications* by J. R. Kenyon (Leicester University Press 1990) and *the English Heritage Book of Castles* by Tom McNeill (Batsford 1992).

CHAPTER 2

Any student of the crusades needs to begin with Sir Steven Runciman's magisterial trilogy: *The First Crusade*, *The Kingdom of Jerusalem* and *The Kingdom of Acre*. All are available as Penguin reprints (2016). Anthony Bridge published a good single volume history, *The Crusades* (Granada 1980), and there's also a range of first-class modern studies: *The Crusades* by Thomas Ashbridge (Simon & Schuster 2012); Christopher Tyerman's *God's War* (Penguin 2007); *Holy Warriors* by Jonathan Phillips (Vintage 2010) and for the battle of Arsuf, Sir Charles Oman is still worth reading – volume one of *The Art of War in the Middle Ages* (Greenhill Press edition 1991), in particular.

CHAPTER 3

This is a snapshot view of a complex subject and we apologize for only being able to offer the battle of Lewes as a one-sentence summary. Readers who wish to know more can refer to the secondary sources listed in the bibliography but for present purposes we've relied on Sir Charles Oman, Dr. D. Carpenter and Dr. Cox. A fuller commentary on and profile of both the contemporary or near-contemporary chronicles and the numerous areas of debate may be found in John Sadler's *The Second Barons' War* published by Pen & Sword in 2008. The quote beginning the chapter – *the murder of Evesham…* – is from Robert of Gloucester, ed. W. A. Wright, II Rolls Service (1887).

CHAPTER 4

For the border wars and border reivers we've relied on mainly secondary sources: G. M. Fraser's *The Steel Bonnets* (Harper Collins 1989 edition); the much earlier *Border Raids and Reivers* by the Reverend J. R Borland, *Ridpath's Border History*, John Sadler's *Border Fury* (Longmans 2004) and his *Raiders and Reivers* (Ergo Press 2006). We've also consulted Tough's *Last Years of a Frontier*, Godfrey Watson's *The Border Reivers*, Royal Commission on Ancient Monument's 1971 *Shielings & Bastles*, John Marsden's *Illustrated Border Ballads* and, of course, Scott's *Minstrelsy*. Two Osprey editions, *Border Reivers* in the "Men-at-Arms" series by Keith Durham and his later *Border Reiver 1513–1603* in the "Elite" series, were also referenced.

CHAPTER 5

Any student of the Hundred Years War should consult Jonathan Sumption's multi-volume history, so far running to four volumes and published by Faber & Faber (1999–2016). John still reveres Colonel A. H. Burne's earlier two-volume series *The Crecy War* (Frontline 2016 reprint) and *The Agincourt War* (Frontline 2014 reprint). Anne Curry has written a good accessible history in the Osprey *Essential History* series, as well as the monograph *Agincourt* (Boydell 2009). Juliet Barker has also produced an excellent study of the battle, *Agincourt* (Abacus 2006). Sir John Keegan writes an interesting section on the battle in his *Face of Battle* (Bodley Head 2014 reprint). Blank verse quotations are from Shakespeare's *Henry V* (Arden Shakespeare 3rd Series 1995).

CHAPTER 6

For this chapter we've relied on primary sources and secondary sources including: Boardman, A.V., *The Battle of Towton* (England 1994); Boardman, A. V., *The Medieval Soldier in the Wars of the Roses* (London 1998); Haigh, P.A., *The Military Campaigns of the Wars of the Roses* (London 1995); Leadman, A.D., *The Battle of Towton* Yorkshire Archaeological Journal vol. 10, (1889); Markham, C., *The Battle of Towton* Yorkshire Archaeological Journal vol. 10, (1889); Ramsay, Sir J.H., *Lancaster and York* 2 vols. (Oxford 1892); Ransome, C., *The Battle of Towton* English Historical Review vol. 4, (1889) and, lastly Sadler D.J. *Palmsunday Field* (England 2011).

CHAPTER 7

Readers who want to take a look at the originals of some of the older sources quoted here should look at *The History of the Kings of Britain* by Geoffrey of Monmouth (Penguin 2015); *Ivanhoe: A Romance* by Sir Walter Scott (New

American Library 1962); *Le Morte D'Arthur* by Sir Thomas Malory (Library of Alexandria 1897) and Roger Lancelyn Green's *King Arthur and the Knights of the Round Table* (Macmillan 2008). You will find an account of the Eglington Tournament in the magnificently titled: *The Eglinton Tournament, and Gentleman Unmasked; In a Conversation Between the Shades of King James V. of Scotland, and Sir David Lindsay of the Mount, Lyon King-at-Arms in the Elysian Fields. By Peter Buchan, Corresponding Member of the Antiquarian Society of Scotland; the Northern Institution for the Promotion of Science and Literature; and the Antiquarian Society of Newcastle-upon-Tyne, &c. &c. &c*, (Simpkin, Marshall, and Company 1840).

PRIMARY SOURCES

A Chronicle of London from 1089 to 1485, ed. H. Nicholas and E. Tyrell (1827)

A Chronicle of the First Thirteen Years of the Reign of Edward IV 1461–1474, J. Warkworth, ed. J. O. Halliwell (1839)

"'A London Chronicle of 1460," ed. G. Baskerville, in *English Historical Review* Vol. XXVIII (1913)

An English Chronicle of the reigns of Richard II, Henry IV, Henry V and Henry VI, ed. J. S. Davies (1856)

"'Annales Rerum Anglicarum," William of Worcester, in *Liber Niger Scaccarii* (2 vols), ed. J. Hearne (1728)

Bishop Percy's Folio Manuscript, Vol. 3, ed. F. J. Furnivall and H. W. Hales (1868)

Brut Chronicle (2 vols), ed. F. W. D. Brie (1906)

Calendar of Documents relating to Scotland Vol. IV 1357–1509, ed. J. Bain (1888)

Calendar of Fine Rolls: Edward IV; Edward V; Richard III, 1471–1485 (1961)

Calendar of Patent Rolls: Edward IV 1467–1477, Edward IV, Edward V, Richard III 1476–1485 (1899–1901)

Calendar of State Papers and Manuscripts existing in the Archives and Collections of Milan, ed. and transl. A. B. Hinds (1912)

"Chronicle of London," W. Gregory, in *Historical Collections of a Citizen of London in the Fifteenth Century*, ed. J. Gairdner (1876)

Chronicles of London, ed. C. L. Kingsford (1905)

Chronicon Adam de Usk, ed. E. M. Thompson (1904)

"Chronique des derniers Ducs de Bourgoyne," G. Chastellain, in *Pantheon Literaire IV* (1827)

Croyland Abbey Chronicle, ed. H. T. Riley (1854)

English Historical Documents Vol. 5 1327–1484, ed. A. R. Myers (1969)

Froissart's Chronicles, ed. G. Brereton (1968)

"Hearne's Fragment," in *Chronicles of the White Rose*, ed. J. A. Giles (1834)

Historiae Regum Anglicae, J. Rous, ed. T. Hearne (1716)

Historie of the Arrivall of King Edward IV in England and the final Recoverye of his Kingdomes from Henry VI A.D. 1471, ed. J. Bruce (1838)

"John Benet's Chronicle for the Years 1400 to 1462," ed. G. L. Hariss and M. A. Harriss, in *Camden Miscellany* Vol. XXIV (London 1972)

Knyghthode and Bataile, ed. R. Dyboski and Z. M. Arend (1935)

Manual of Sword-fighting, H. Talhoffer, ed. and transl. M. Rector (2000)

Plumpton Letters, ed. T. Stapleton (1839)

Recueil des Chroniques D'Angleterre, J. de Waurin, ed. W. Hardy and E. L. C. P. Hardy (1891)

"Registrum," J. Whethamstede, in *Registra quorandum Abbatum Monasterii S. Albani* (2 vols), ed. H. Riley (1872–1873)

Registrum Abbatis Johannis Whethamstede, ed. H. T. Riley (1872)

"Rose of Rouen," *Archaeologia* XXIX pp. 344–347 (1842)

Rotuli. Parliamentorum (6 vols), ed. J. Strachey *et al.* (1767–1777)

Scottish Exchequer Rolls VII Ramsay ii

Short English Chronicle, ed. J. Gairdner (1880)

The Cotton Manuscripts. The British Library

The Croyland Chronicle Continuation 1459–1486, ed. N. Prona and J. Cox (1986)

The Great Chronicle of London, ed. A. H. Thomas and I. D. Thornley (1938)

The Harleian Manuscripts (4 vols), ed. P. W. Hammond and R. Horrox (1979–1983)

The History of Richard III, Sir T. More, ed. R. S. Sylvester (1963)

The Memoirs of the Reign of Louis XI 1461–1463, P. de Commynes, transl. M. Jones (1972)

The Household of Edward IV, ed. A. R. Myers (1959)

The New Chronicles of England and France, R. Fabyan, ed. H. Ellis (1809)

The Paston Letters 1422–1509 (3 vols), ed. J. Gairdner (1872–1875)

The Priory of Hexham Vol. I (1864)

The Rous Roll, J. Rous, ed. C. Ross and W. Courthope (1980)

'The Year Book de *Termino Paschae* 4 Edward IV', in *Priory of Hexham, S.S.* 1 (1864)

The Union of the Two Noble and Illustre Famelies of Lancastre and York, E. Hall (1548)

The Usurpation of Richard III, D. Mancini, ed. C. A. J. Armstrong (1969)

Three Books of Polydore Vergil's English History, ed. H. Ellis (1844)

Three Fifteenth Century Chronicles, ed. J. Gairdner (1880)

York Records of the Fifteenth Century, ed. R. Davies (1843)

SECONDARY SOURCES

Allen, K., *The Wars of the Roses* (London 1973)

Allmand, C., *Henry V* (London 1992)

Archer, R. E. C., *Government and people in the Fifteenth Century* (England 1995)

Arthurson, I., *The Perkin Warbeck Conspiracy 1491–1499* (England 1977)

Attreed, L. (ed.), *York House Books* (England 1991)

Bagley, J. J., *Margaret of Anjou, Queen of England* (London 1948)

Bain, J. (ed.), *Calendar of Documents Relating to Scotland 1108–1509* (Edinburgh 1881–1888)

Barbour, R., *The Knight and Chivalry* (London 1974)

Barnard, F., *Edward IV French Expedition* (London 1975)

Bartlett, C., *The English Longbowman 1313–1515* (England 1995)

Bates, C. J., *History of Northumberland* (London 1895)

Bennet, M., *The Battle of Bosworth* (New York 1985)

Bennet, M., *Lambert Simnel and the Battle of Stoke* (England 1987)

Bingham, C., *The Stewart Kings of Scotland 1371–1603* (London 1974)

Blackmore, H. L., *The Armouries of the Tower of London – Ordnance* (HMSO 1976)

Blair, C., *European Armour* (London 1958)

Boardman, A. V., *The Battle of Towton* (England 1994)

Boardman, A. V., *The Medieval Soldier in the Wars of the Roses* (London 1998)

Burne, Colonel A. H., *Battlefields of England* (London 1950)

Burne, Colonel A. H., *More Battlefields of England* (London 1952)

Carpenter C., *The Wars of the Roses: Politics and the Constitution in England c. 1437–1509* (Cambridge 2002)

Carpenter, D., *The Battles of Lewes and Evesham 1264–1265* (England 1987)

Carpenter, D., Simon de Montfort and the Mise of Lewes, in *Bulletin of the Institute of Historical Research* LVIII (1985)

Carpenter, D., What happened in 1258?, in *War and Government in the Middle Ages: Essays in Honour of J.O. Prestwich*, ed. J. Gillingham and J. C. Holt (Woodbridge, 1984)

Chrimes, S. B., *Henry VII* (London 1952)

Clive, M., *The Sun of York, Edward IV* (London 1973)

Cole, H., *The Wars of the Roses* (London 1973)

Cook, D. R., *Lancastrians & Yorkists, The Wars of the Roses* (London 1984)

Coward, B., *The Stanleys, Lord Stanley and Earls of Derby 1385–1672* (England 1983)

Cox, D.C., *The Battle of Evesham. A New Account* (The Vale of Evesham Historical Society 1988)

Cockray, K. R., The Yorkshire Rebellions of 1469, in *The Ricardian* Vol. 6 No. 82 (December 1983)

Dockray, K. R., *Chronicles of the Reign of Edward IV* (England 1983)

Ducklin, K. and J. Waller, *Sword Fighting* (London 2001)

Falkus, G., *The Life and Times of Edward IV* (London 1981)

Fiorato, V., A Boylston and C. Knussel (eds), *Blood and Roses: The Archaeology of a Mass Grave from the Battle of Towton AD 1461* (Oxford 2000)

Foss, P. J., *The Field of Redemore Plain: The Battle of Bosworth* (England 1990)

Gairdner, J. (ed.), *The Paston Letters* (England 1986)

Gillingham, J., *The Wars of the Roses* (London 2001)

Green, V. H. H., *The Later Plantagenets* (London 1955)

Goodman, A., *The Wars of the Roses* (London 1981)

Gravett, C., *Medieval Siege Warfare* (England 1990)

Griffiths, R. A., *Kings and Nobles in the Later Middle Ages* (England 1986)

Haigh, P. A., *The Battle of Wakefield* (England 1996)

Haigh, P. A., *The Military Campaigns of the Wars of the Roses* (London 1995)

Hallam, E., *The Plantagenet Encyclopaedia* (London 1990)

Hallam, E. (ed.), *The Chronicles of the Wars of the Roses* (London 1988)

Hammond, P. W., *Richard III – Lordship Loyalty and Law* (England 1986)

Hammond, P. W., *The Battles of Barnet and Tewkesbury* (New York 1990)

Hammond, P. W. and A. Sutton, *Richard III – The Road to Bosworth Field* (London 1985)

Harvey, J., *The Plantagenets* (London 1948)

Hepple, L. W., *A History of Northumberland and Newcastle upon Tyne* (London 1976)

Hibbert, C., *Agincourt* (London 1964)

Hicks, M.A., Edward IV, The Duke of Somerset and Lancastrian Loyalism in the North, in *Northern History* Vol. 20 (1984)

Hicks, M. A., *False, Fleeting Perjur'd Clarence, George Duke of Clarence* (England 1980)

Hicks, M. A., Warwick; The Reluctant Kingmaker, in *Medieval History* Vol. 1 No. 2 (1991)

Hodges, G., *Ludford Bridge and Mortimer's Cross* (England 1988)

Horrox, R., *Richard III – A Study in Service* (England 1989)

Johnson, P. A., *Richard, Duke of York 1411–1460* (London 1988)

Keegan, J., *The Face of Battle* (London 1976)

Keen, M., *English Society in the Later Middle Ages 1348–1500* (England 1990)

Keen, M. (ed.), *Medieval Warfare – a History* (Oxford 1999)

Kendall, P. M., *Warwick the Kingmaker* (New York 1957)

Kendall, P. M., *Richard III* (New York 1955)

Kendall, P. M., *The Wars of the Roses* (New York 1957)

Kipling, R., Arithmetic on the Frontier, in *Departmental Ditties and Other Verses*, (England 1886)

Jones, M. K., *Bosworth 1485 – The Psychology of a Battle* (England 2002)

Lander, J. R., *The Wars of the Roses* (London 1990)

Lomas, R., *North-East England in The Middle Ages* (Edinburgh 1992)

Long, B., *The Castles of Northumberland* (Newcastle-upon-Tyne 1967)

Lynch, M., *A New History of Scotland* (London 1991)

McFarlane, K. B., *The Nobility of Late Medieval England* (Oxford 1975)

McFarlane, K. B., *England in the Fifteenth Century*, ed. G.L. Harris (London 1981)

McFarlane, K. B., The Wars of the Roses, in *Proceedings of the British Academy* (50 1964)

Mortimer, I., *The Greatest Traitor* (London 2003)

Myers, A. R. (ed.), *The Household of Edward IV: The Black Book and the Ordinance of 1478* (England 1950)

Neillands, R., *The Hundred Years War* (London 1990)

Neillands, R., *The Wars of the Roses* (London 1992)

Nicolle, D., *Medieval Warfare Source Book* (London 1999)

Norman, A.V.B. and D. Pottinger, *English Weapons and Warfare 449–1660* (London 1966)

Oakeshott, R. E., *A Knight and his Weapons* (London 1964)

Oman, Sir C., *The Art of War in the Middle Ages* vol. 2 (London 1924)

Pollard, A. J., Percies, Nevilles and the Wars of the Roses, in *History Today* (September 1992)

Prestwich, M., *Armies and Warfare in the Middle Ages* (London 1996)

Ramsay, Sir J. H., *Lancaster and York* 2 vols. (Oxford 1892)

Ransome, C., The Battle of Towton, *English Historical Review* vol. 4, (1889)

Ridpath, G., *The Border History of England and Scotland* (Berwick upon Tweed 1776)

Roberts, D., *The Battle of Stoke* (England 1987)

Rogers, Col. H. C. B., *Artillery Through the Ages* (London 1971)

Rose, A., *Kings in the North* (London 2002)

Rowse, A.L., *Bosworth Field and the War of the Roses* (London 1966)

Runciman, Sir S., *The Fall of Constantinople* (England 1965)

Sadler, D. J., *War in the North – The Wars of the Roses in the North East of England 1461–1464* (England 2000)

Sadler, D. J., *Border Fury – The Three Hundred Years War* (England 2004)

Seward, D., *Henry V as Warlord* (London 1987)

Seward, D., *Richard III – England's Black Legend* (England 1983)

Seward, D., *The Wars of the Roses* (London 1995)

Seymour, W., *Battles in Britain* vol. 1, (London 1989)

Smurthwaite, D., *The Ordnance Survey Guide to the Battlefields of Britain* (London 1984)

Tough, D. L. W., *The Last Years of a Frontier* (Oxford 1928)

Trevelyan, G. M., *A History of England* (London 1926)

Tuck, A., *Crown and Nobility, 1272–1462* (England 1985)

Wagner, P., and Hand, S., *Medieval Sword and Shield* (California 2003)

Warner, P., *Sieges of the Middle Ages* (London 1968)

Wise, T., *Medieval Heraldry* (England 1980)

Wise, T., *The Wars of the Roses* (London 1983)

Wolffe, B., *Henry VI* (London 1981)

Woolgar, C. M., *The Great Household in late Medieval England* (London 1999)

ACKNOWLEDGEMENTS

Chivalry is an emotive title, particularly for the generation brought up on '50s and early '60s children's TV programs such as *Knights of the Round Table, Robin Hood* (the Richard Greene version, of course), *William Tell* and, not to be forgotten, *Ivanhoe* – Roger Moore in his pre-"Saint" days. These went in tandem with reading the glorious Puffin of *Knights of the Round Table* by Roger Lancelyn Green, the novels of Rosemary Sutcliff, Henry Treece, G.A. Henty; Stevenson and Dumas. Knighthood, the virtues of chivalry, were paramount; the medieval tradition carried forward by Biggles, Beau Geste and Karl the Viking.

Thanks are due firstly to Ruth Sheppard, our editor at Casemate, Dr. Maureen Meikle of Leeds University, Dr. Richard Britnell of Durham University, Professor Tony Pollard of the University of Teesside; to our colleagues at the former Centre for Lifelong Learning, Sunderland University, particularly Colm O'Brien and Max Adams, to Chloe Rodham for producing the maps and battle plans, Ed Wimble, Catherine Turner of Durham Cathedral Library, Iain Dickie and Michael Rayner of the Battlefields Trust, Tony Whiting of Evesham Tourist Centre, John Wollaston, Beryl Charlton and particularly to Tony Spicer who was most generous with his research. Yet again thanks are due to Adam Barr for the photography, Robert Hardy CBE, Richard Groocock of the National Archives, Dr. David Caldwell of the National Museum of Scotland, Christopher Burgess, Alistair Bowden of "Remembering Flodden," Dr. Tobias Capwell of the Wallace Collection, Clive Hallam-Baker, Fiona Armstrong of the Armstrong Trust and Heritage Centre, Dr. Gillian Scott of the Castles Study Group, Dr. Ian Roberts of North Tyne Heritage Centre, Jennifer Gill and Liz Bregazzi of the County Durham Record Office, Malin Holst of the Towton Mass Grave Project, Philip Albert and John Waller of Royal Armouries, Nicola Waghorn of the National Gallery, Matthew Bailey of the National Portrait Gallery, the staff of the Lit. & Phil. Library at Newcastle-upon-Tyne, Adrian Waite of the Red Wyverns, Duncan Brown of EH Photo Library, Anthea Boylston and Jo Buckberry of Bradford University, Winnie Tyrell of Glasgow Museums, Mark Taylor and Graham Darbyshire of Towton Battlefield Society, Bob Brooks of Hotspur School of Defence, Paul MacDonald of MacDonald Armouries.

Any errors and omissions remain entirely the responsibility of the authors. We have, at all times attempted to fully identify current copyright holders. If we have failed to do so in any instance we should be glad to hear from and will amend our text accordingly.

Rosie Serdiville & John Sadler
Northumberland/Newcastle-upon-Tyne, 2017

INDEX

Agnes, Countess of Dunbar; 60–62
Alexander III, King of Scotland; 79
Archibald, earl of Eglington; 138

Balliol, John King of Scotland; 79–81
Battles –
- Acre 1291; 59
- Agincourt 1415; 17; 101–105
- Alnwick 1174; 20
- Arsuf 1191; 57–58
- Bannockburn 1314; 21, 32
- Bosworth 1485; 132, 134
- Castillon 1453; 115
- Crecy 1346; 77, 96–97
- Dupplin Moor 1332; 81
- Evesham 1265; 9, 68–70
- Falkirk 1298; 21
- Flodden 1513; 85
- Halidon Hill 1333; 82, 95
- Hexham 1464; 132
- Lake Manzikert 1071; 46
- Lewes 1263; 61, 62
- Najera 1366; 98
- Neville's Cross 1346; 82
- Patay 1429; 136
- Pinkie 1547; 81
- Poitiers 1356; 77
- Rouvray ('Battle of the Herrings')
  1429; 136
- Sluys 1340; 96
- Towton 1461; 21; 116–128
- Visby 1361; 21
Beaufort, Henry Cardinal; 108–110
Beaufort, Henry 2nd Duke; 116
Beaufort, Henry 3rd Duke; 121–128
Bloody Meadow; 21

Castles –
- Alnwick; 34
- Arundel; 34
- Bamburgh; 34
- Beziers; 39

- Edinburgh; 34
- Framlingham; 34
- Gilnockie; 34
- Kenilworth; 66
- Kidwelly; 92
- Neidpath; 34
- Newcastle; 34
- Orford; 34; 36
- Rochester; 34, 63
- Stirling; 34, 39
- Smailholm; 34
Charles V; 114
Charles VII of France; 110–111
Clifford, Lord John ("the Butcher"); 19,
  117–119
Conrad II of Germany; 49

David II, King of Scotland; 82
De Montfort, Henry; 75
De Montfort, Simon, the Elder; 9, 14,
  63–68
De Montfort, Simon, the Younger;
  64–66
De Mowbray, John, 3rd Duke of
  Norfolk; 129–130
De Vivar, Rodrigo Diaz; 45
"Disinherited," the; 81–83
Douglas, James 2nd Earl; 43, 44

Edward I of England; 9, 11, 31, 39, 63–68
Edward III of England; 9, 38, 81, 95
Edward IV of England; 116, 117–128
Edward, the Black Prince; 77, 98–99
Erpingham, Sir Thomas; 101
Excalibur; 15

"Flower of Craven," the; 118
Forster, Sir John; 86
Frederick ("Barbarossa"); 52

Godfrey of Bouillon; 47
Gordon, General Charles; 6, 7

Gurdon, Adam; 33
Guy of Lusignan; 51
Gwenllian ferch Gruffydd; 91–93

Harold II, King of England; 31
Hawkwood, Sir John; 77–79
Henry I of England; 40
Henry II of England; 7, 36
Henry III of England; 62
Henry IV of England; 99
Henry V of England; 94–95; 99–105,
    109
Henry VI of England; 106, 110–111,
    117, 123, 126, 132
Henry VII of England; 131, 134
Henry VIII of England; 85, 140
Henry Percy ("Hotspur"); 42, 43
Henry Percy, 3rd Earl of
    Northumberland; 124–127
Hobilars; 80
Hugh of Burgundy; 58
Humphrey, Duke of Gloucester; 109

James I of Scotland; 82
James IV of Scotland; 85, 140
James V of Scotland; 90
Joan of Arc; 115, 135–136
John, Duke of Bedford; 106
John, King of England; 27

King Arthur; 139–140
Knights Templar; 11

Lambton, Sir John; 17
Llewellyn; 64
Louis VII of France; 49

Margaret of Anjou; 110
Mary, Queen of Scots; 90
Matilda, Queen of England; 25

Neville Richard, Earl of Warwick,
    ("the Kingmaker"); 116
Neville, William, Lord Fauconberg;
    117–119

Peter the Hermit; 47
Philip Augustus, King of France; 53–55
Philip IV of France; 96

Raymond, Count of Toulouse; 47
Reynald of Chatillon; 50
Richard I of England ("Lionheart"); 26;
    53–58
Richard III of England; 132–134
Richard de la Pole, Duke of Suffolk;
    109–111
Richard, Duke of York; 115
Robert I, King of Scotland ('the Bruce');
    32; 80–81
Robert II of Normandy; 47
Robert de Bohemond; 47

Saladin; 50, 51, 55–57
Steel Bonnets; 80
Stephen, King of England; 25, 38

Treaty of Bretigny; 77
Trollope, Andrew; 123–126

Urban II; 44

Von Berlichingen, Gotz; 112–114

Wallace, William ("Braveheart"); 80–82
Weardale Campaign 1326; 9
Wilfred of Ivanhoe; 142–144
William I of England; 31, 79
William the Lion, King of Scotland; 20
William the Marshal; 25, 26, 27, 32
White Company; 77